Count Me In:
Jewish Wisdom in Action

Gila Gevirtz

Editorial Committee
Rabbi Martin Cohen
Rabbi Daniel Levin
Julie Vanek, R.J.E.

Behrman House Publishers
www.behrmanhouse.com

Book and Cover Design: **Russell Cohen**

Illustrations: **Bob Wakelin**

Project Manager: **Gila Gevirtz**

The publisher gratefully acknowledges the cooperation of the following sources of photographs and graphic images:

Kathy Bloomfield 92; **Creative Image** 12 top, 13, 54, 61, 64, 92 (top), 100, 101, 103, 110 (top); **Gustav Doré** 49 (top), 132 (top); **Gila Gevirtz** 8, 12 (bottom), 16, 24 (bottom), 25, 30, 36, 39, 47, 50, 58, 64, 66, 72, 77, 82, 86–87, 88, 102, 113, 121, 128, 132 (bottom); **Israel Ministry of Tourism** 5, 51, 60 (bottom), 110–111 (bottom), 120; **Terry Kaye** 32, 34, 40, 60 (top), 86, 111 (top), 124, 125; **Francine Keery** 76; **Richard Lobell** 10, 14, 46, 52, 90, 98, 106, 112, 123; **Hara Person** 115, 134–135; **Ginny Twersky** 4 (top), 26, 38, 62, 74, 75; **Therese Wagner** 8; **Vicki Weber** 122.

The publisher and author gratefully acknowledge Seymour Rossel for his editorial contributions.

Published by Behrman House, Inc.
Springfield, NJ 07081
www.behrmanhouse.com

Library of Congress Cataloging-in-Publication Data

Gevirtz, Gila.
  Count me in : Jewish wisdom in action / Gila Gevirtz.
      p. cm.
  Includes index.
  ISBN 0-87441-194-7 (alk. paper)
  1. Jewish ethics--Juvenile literature. 2. Jewish way of life--Juvenile literature.
  3. Jewish religious education--Textbooks for children. I. Title.

BJ1285.G48 2005
296.7--dc22

2004017578

Dedicated to three great gals, Ada Truppin, Rhoda Krawitz, and Valerie Pinhas.

—G.G.

Contents

What does this book have to do with the *really* important questions in your life?

Let's face it, you're smart and you already know a lot. You know that Shabbat is a day of rest and that Passover celebrates the liberation of our people from Egypt. You know that Hebrew is the sacred language of the Jews and that we believe in one God.

Every day you learn new stuff—not only about Judaism, science, math, and English, but also about yourself and other people. You learn what makes you happy, sad, or impatient. You learn who your loyal friends are and what their favorite sports are. And you learn how to become more independent and responsible. But sometimes, the more you learn, the more questions you have. For example, you may find yourself wondering: If my best friend and I don't like the same music, can we really be friends? Do all families argue like mine? Do I need to care about people I don't like? Why must I be polite even when I don't feel like it?

Such questions are important. Over the centuries, others who were searching for the truth asked the same questions. Among these seekers were the sages of Israel—the ancient rabbis, who studied the Bible and helped future generations find answers to their questions. True, much of what they wrote helps us observe Jewish holy days and rituals, but even more of their teachings help us figure out how to take care of ourselves, get along with others, and live lives that we can be proud of.

Count Me In: Jewish Wisdom in Action will introduce you to how the wisdom of our sages can help answer your important questions. The more you *learn*, the better you can use Jewish wisdom to strengthen yourself and others. The more you *practice* what you learn, the greater your success will be in both helping the Jewish people make the world a better place and in living the best life you can.

כָּל שֶׁחָכְמָתוֹ מְרֻבָּה מִמַּעֲשָׂיו, לְמַה הוּא דוֹמֶה? לְאִילָן שֶׁעֲנָפָיו מְרֻבִּין וְשָׁרָשָׁיו מוּעָטִין, וְהָרוּחַ בָּאָה וְעוֹקַרְתּוֹ וְהוֹפַכְתּוֹ עַל פָּנָיו:

Rabbi Elazar ben Azariah taught, "Those whose wisdom is greater than their deeds, to what may they be compared? To trees whose branches are many but whose roots are few. The wind comes and uproots and overturns them."
—*Pirkei Avot* 3:17

WISDOM AND
Action

Two Talumdic sages, Rabbi Tarfon and Rabbi Akiva, struggled to determine which is more important—the study of Torah or living according to its laws, God's *mitzvot*. Rabbi Tarfon was convinced that it is more important to follow the laws of Torah. Rabbi Akiva argued that the only way to know what the laws are is to study Torah.

In the end, the sages determined that the study of Torah is greater than all other *mitzvot* because it leads to them all.

—Talmud, *Kiddushin* 40b

• •

Why do you go to religious school? Because your parents want you to? To learn what you need to know for your bar or bat mitzvah service or confirmation? Because your best friend goes and you want to be together?

These are all good reasons. But what you may not know is that through your participation you strengthen a tradition—and a dream—that has inspired generations.

OUR SACRED
Covenant

Centuries ago, before supersonic jets, digital cameras, and DVD players were invented, before the United States was a nation, and before the first word of English was spoken, the Jewish people had a dream. It was an awesome dream of a world ruled by justice, truth, and mercy—a world filled with hope and kindness, in which all creatures lived in harmony and peace.

Centuries before there were Hebrew words for conveniences such as cell phones, cars, and computers, there were Hebrew words for values such as justice, truth, and mercy.

The Torah teaches that to help make that dream come true, our ancestors entered into an agreement with God. The agreement is called the *Brit*, or Covenant. Through the *Brit*, God promises to make the Jewish people a holy nation if they fulfill God's sacred commandments, or *mitzvot*. When our ancestors made the Covenant with God, they made it for themselves, their children, their children's children, and all generations of Jews after them—then, now, and forever.

For over three thousand years, the Jewish people have worked to honor the Covenant. In fact, each time you fulfill a mitzvah—such as comforting someone who is ill, feeding the hungry, or participating in Shabbat and holiday prayer services—you honor the *Brit* and bring our people's dream of a just and peaceful world a little closer to reality.

Among your dreams might be the desire to marry when you grow up. How might your religious school studies help you reach this goal by guiding you to make wise choices along the way?

OUR SACRED
Teachings

The Bible

Our holy teachings—which include the Bible and the wisdom of our ancient teachers, the sages—help us

THE BOOKS OF THE BIBLE

The Bible (Tanach) includes the five books of the Pentateuch (Torah), the nineteen books of the Prophets (Nevi'im), and the twelve books of Writings (K'tuvim). The Torah, sometimes called the Five Books of Moses, includes the books of Genesis (B'reishit), Exodus (Sh'mot), Leviticus (Vayikra), Numbers (B'midbar), and Deuteronomy (D'varim).

understand God's *mitzvot* and provide instructions for fulfilling them. They explain the values—the specific beliefs and actions, such as belief in one God and acts of lovingkindness—that form the foundation of Judaism.

The Torah teaches the early story of the Jewish people. By studying it, we learn much about our tradition and the values that guide Jewish life. From Abraham and Sarah, we learn the mitzvah of welcoming guests, *hachnasat orḥim*. Their model of hospitality teaches us to be gracious hosts. Serving a friend a meal of pizza and salad is one way to honor this Jewish tradition.

What Are Your Dreams?

Do you have dreams of who you will be and what your life will be like when you grow up? Perhaps you dream of becoming a scientist, a writer, a professional athlete, or a teacher. Maybe you dream of living in a foreign country, in a big city skyscraper, or on a secluded island.

Describe three hopes and dreams for your future.

1. _____
   _____

2. _____
   _____

3. _____
   _____

What can you do to help make your dreams come true?

_____
_____
_____
_____

How can what you learn in religious school help you succeed?

_____
_____
_____
_____

After you have completed this book, you may want to come back to this activity, review your answers, and perhaps add to or change them.

From Moses, we learn the value of leadership, and from his sister, Miriam, the importance of concern for family. At a time when the Israelites were oppressed, Moses bravely led them out of Egypt toward the Promised Land. That act made him the greatest leader in all Jewish history.

Today we can develop our own leadership skills—for example, by organizing mitzvah projects and leading prayer services. And just as Miriam watched over baby Moses while he lay in a basket on the Nile River, so can we show concern for family by looking after younger siblings or helping our parents when they are tired or ill.

From the many *mitzvot* described in the Torah, we learn the values of caring for all of God's creations, honoring our parents, and treating others with dignity, honesty, and fairness. Those *mitzvot* help us figure out what is selfish and what is fair, when we need to work hard and when we need to rest. They encourage us to think before we act and to act with respect for ourselves and others.

In addition to the Torah, we study the other sacred texts of the Bible, including the

THE GIVING OF THE TORAH

The Book of Exodus tells the story of the giving of the Torah on Mount Sinai.

Early in the morning on the appointed day, Moses led the Israelites to the foot of Mount Sinai. The mountain was surrounded by thick clouds and smoke, and the crash of thunder rumbled and roared across the sky. The Israelites stood in awe as bolts of lightning streaked the heavens with the sharpness of a knife and the blast of a shofar, a ram's horn, grew louder and louder.

Then, as suddenly as the deafening sounds had come, they stopped. All was silent.

The Torah tells us that God spoke and the Israelites received the Ten Commandments.

After the Ten Commandments were given, Moses received the other laws of Torah from God. And Moses taught the *mitzvot* to the children of Israel so that they could become a holy people, an *am kadosh*.

The holiday of Shavuot, which is observed in the spring, celebrates the giving of the Torah. In Hebrew, the holiday is called Z'man Matan Torateinu, meaning "the Time of the Giving of Our Torah." Why does the name refer only to the giving of the Torah and not to the receiving of the Torah? Because the Torah was given only once, centuries ago, but it is received every day. Every day each Jew can receive the Torah by studying it and observing *mitzvot*. Every day each Jew can receive the Torah by struggling to figure out how to apply its lessons and laws to daily life.

What action will you take to receive the Torah today?

_____

_____

_____

Every Shabbat we read a portion of the Torah as part of the prayer service. We also read from the Torah during prayer services on Mondays and Thursdays.

books of the Prophets. From the prophets Isaiah and Hosea, we learn to observe holy days and rituals. However, these prophets teach us that fulfilling those *mitzvot* has value only if we also observe the *mitzah* of treating one another with kindness and generosity.

From the prophet Elijah, we learn that although God didn't make Jews different from others, there are times when Jews must behave differently to honor the *Brit*. For example, though the laws of many countries make it illegal to treat animals cruelly, they do not require citizens to help animals in need. In contrast, because compassion for all God's creatures is a basic Jewish value, Jewish law requires that we provide cold and hungry animals with shelter and food, that we permit animals to rest on Shabbat, and that we feed pets before we feed ourselves.

The third section of the Bible, Writings, also teaches us values. For example, from the Scroll of Esther (Megillat Esther), we learn the values of courage and loyalty to community. And from the Book of Psalms (T'hilim), a collection of religious poems and prayers, we learn the values of justice and peace, love and trust in God and Torah, and respect for human life.

Knowing what you know about Jewish values, do you think that fishing and hunting for sport rather than for food reflect Jewish values? Why or why not?

The Talmud

In addition to the lessons of the Bible, our tradition includes the Talmud, a series of sacred books that contain Jewish law, or *halachah*. Included in the Talmud are the discussions, opinions, and stories of our ancient rabbis, or sages, that explain in more detail how we can

THE WRITTEN LAW AND THE ORAL LAW

The Bible is often called the Written Law. In contrast, the Talmud, which is the legal commentaries on the Bible, is often called the Oral Law.

Originally the Oral Law was passed by word of mouth from teachers to students, from one generation to the next. However, the Mishnah (the earliest portion of the Talmud) was written down in about 200 CE by Rabbi Yehudah Hanasi (Judah the Prince) to make sure that its lessons and laws would not be lost. Rabbi Yehudah and the rabbis who worked with him tried to record all they had learned from their teachers, including laws about how to buy and sell things, how to celebrate holidays, how to marry, and how to establish a court.

The Gemara (the later portion of the Talmud that records the rabbinic commentaries on the Mishnah as well as stories, Torah commentaries, rituals, and prayers) was written down in about 500 CE.

We read Megillat Esther on the holiday of Purim. Unlike the Torah scroll, which has a roller on each side, the Scroll of Esther has only one roller.

honor the *Brit*. For example, Leviticus 19:14 teaches, "You shall not insult the deaf or place a stumbling block before the blind," but it is the Talmud that explains that this means we should not mislead people or take advantage of them.

Through the lessons of the Talmud, the ancient rabbis teach us how *mitzvot* and Jewish values can help us gain wisdom—and use it to raise children, run businesses, build communities, and spend our leisure time. They help us understand how to honor the *Brit* on weekdays and holy days, through each season of the year and each season of our lives, from youth through old age.

Our families and teachers pass on Jewish wisdom and tradition in many ways—by teaching us Hebrew and Bible stories, reciting blessings over us on Friday nights, and treating us with love and respect.

LEARN IT &
Live It

How do you know how well you've succeeded in your study of Jewish sacred texts and values? How do you know whether you've grown in your wisdom?

In secular school, if you study your social studies or history textbook, pay attention in class, do your assignments, and score above 90 on your tests, you will probably ace the subject. If you take a math test and all of your answers are right, you will score 100 percent. Though tests and grades certainly aren't the only ways to measure your success and growth, they usually play an important role.

But religious school is different. Tests and grades cannot fully measure your success and growth as a student of Jewish tradition and as a partner in the *Brit*. So religious schools measure your success and growth based on the lessons you put into practice, for only when you live them does it matter that you learned them.

For example, when you study the Jewish holidays and use your knowledge to give tzedakah to those in need on Purim, to appreciate how lucky you are to be free on Passover, and to ask family and friends for forgiveness on Yom Kippur, you know that your wisdom has grown. And when you study the Bible and use its lessons of caring for God's creations to teach you to recycle paper, show kindness to animals, honor your parents, and treat yourself and others with respect, you know that your wisdom has grown.

As a Jew, you become wiser and more successful each time you put those Jewish values into action. To know the names of the letters and sounds of the *alef bet* is not enough. To have true wisdom, you must use your knowledge to help fulfill the Covenant. And a knowledge of the lessons a Bible story teaches is not enough. To be successful, you need to use that knowledge to help you perform acts of lovingkindness, generosity, and compassion.

PIRKEI AVOT

Pirkei Avot is one of the sixty-three short books, or tractates, that make up the Talmud. Unlike the other tractates, *Pirkei Avot* does not include any laws. Instead, the rabbis decided to collect the most famous sayings and advice they had learned from their teachers.

They included the wisdom of more than sixty sages who lived in the period from approximately 300 BCE to 200 CE. *Pirkei Avot* explores some of the most important Jewish values and teaches how they can guide our everyday lives.

From Generation to Generation

One of Judaism's most sacred values is to pass Jewish wisdom and tradition from one generation to the next. *Pirkei Avot* teaches that "Moses received the Torah at Sinai and handed it down to Joshua; Joshua to the elders; and the elders to the prophets. And the prophets handed it down to the men of the great assembly" (1:1).

Now it is your turn to receive those sacred teachings. Study them, and let their wisdom teach you how to live a good life. For some day you will be called on to hand them over to the next generation—perhaps with the addition of your own bit of wisdom.

Not only does the Talmud teach us not to "place a stumbling block before the blind," but it also teaches us to help those in need. We study these lessons, then look for opportunities to practice them.

As you read *Count Me In: Jewish Wisdom in Action*, you will encounter the wisdom of many ancient and modern Jewish sages, including Moses, the daughters of Tz'lafeḥad, Rabbi Akiva, Hillel, Henrietta Szold, Albert Einstein, and Rebecca Gratz. You will discover how ordinary human beings can accomplish extraordinary good through the sacred acts of feeding the poor, healing the sick, and working to end human suffering and oppression. And you will learn how you can contribute to that good.

You will learn about many Jewish values, though not every Jewish value—even a lifetime of study may not be enough time for that. However, you will discover that all you need to do is your part. You needn't be perfect, just persistent in your effort to grow and improve.

As a member of the *Brit*, you have a share in the hopes and dreams of our people. You have a part to play in making the world a better place. And each time you put Jewish wisdom into action, it is as if you were standing at Mount Sinai, saying, "*Hineni!* Here I am. Count me in."

נֵר־לְרַגְלִי דְבָרֶךָ וְאוֹר לִנְתִיבָתִי:

Your word is a lamp unto my feet, a light for my path.
—Psalm 119:63

16

HINENI:
COUNT ME IN!

Hineni is a Hebrew word that means "here I am." The Book of Genesis teaches that our patriarch Abraham answered *"hineni"* when God called on him to leave his father's house and follow God's command. By answering *hineni*, it was as if Abraham were saying, "Count me in, God. I'm ready to serve You."

Generations later God called to Moses from the burning bush. As Abraham did, Moses responded *"hineni"* and served God by leading the Israelites out of Egypt, to Mount Sinai, and toward the Promised Land. Then, generations later, the prophet Samuel expressed his own readiness to serve when he, too, said *"hineni."*

And so our tradition continues with you, your family, your community, and Jewish communities around the world. Each time you take a sacred action to help fulfill the *Brit,* it is as if you have said, *"Hineni! Count me in!"*

חָבִיב אָדָם שֶׁנִּבְרָא בְצֶלֶם: חִבָּה יְתֵרָה נוֹדַעַת לוֹ שֶׁנִּבְרָא בְצֶלֶם:

Rabbi Akiva taught, "Beloved is humankind, for we were created in the image of God, but it was by a special love that it was made known to us that we were created in the image of God."

—*Pirkei Avot* 3:14

THE VALUE OF Life

A Ḥasidic sage taught that every person should have two pockets: "In one pocket there should be a piece of paper saying, 'I am but dust and ashes,' When you are feeling proud, reach into that pocket, take out the note, and read it.

"In the other pocket there should be a piece of paper saying, 'For my sake the world was created.' When you are feeling unhappy and lowly, reach into that pocket, take out the note, and read it."

Yesterday, at the end of the day, into which pocket might you have reached? Why? Did you feel different this morning or this afternoon? Which pocket would you have reached into then?

Sometimes when our moods change, particularly because of a success or a failure, our feelings about ourselves change. For example, you may receive an A on a science project and feel like a million dollars but an hour later miss a basketball free throw and groan, "I feel *so* worthless."

Does the value of a person actually change from hour to hour or from day to day? Or is it only the person's feelings that change?

It's easy to feel like a winner when we succeed, but no one can succeed all of the time. That's why it's important for us to value the effort itself. When we try our best, win or lose, we have much to be proud of.

IN THE
Image of God

Our tradition teaches that "one person is equal to the whole of Creation" (*Avot de Rabbi Natan* 31). It does not instruct us that only a great scholar or a powerful ruler is equal to the whole of Creation or that an uneducated or poor person is worth a lesser amount. No! Jewish tradition teaches that *every* person is equal to the whole of Creation.

That teaching is based on the Torah's statement that "God created the human being in God's image, *b'tzelem Elohim*" (Genesis 1:27). But what, you may ask, does "made in God's image" mean? People look so different from one another. Some of us are extremely tall, some short; some have dark skin, others light complexions; some of us are women, others are men. And none of us has the exact same fingerprints, voice, or eyes. If we are so different, how can all of us be made in God's image? And if we are made in God's image, does that mean that God has arms, a mouth, and eyes?

The Torah provides a clue: "God made the human being from the dust of the earth and breathed the breath of life into the human's nostrils, and the human became a living soul" (Genesis 2:7). That verse teaches us that although humans are made of earthly matter—skin, bones, flesh, and blood—each of us has a spark of the divine in us, for the breath of God flows through every human being in the form of a soul, or spirit. And just as God is invisible, so is the human soul.

According to Jewish tradition, our souls help us live as creatures made in God's image. Just as the earthly organs within us—our hearts, lungs, and brains—enable us to live busy lives filled with rewarding activities such as playing musical instruments, writing computer programs,

Ancient Stories for Modern Times

ZUSYA'S LESSON

Because each of us has the potential to add goodness to the world, all we need do is strive to become our best selves. Rabbi Zusya of Hanipol taught that lesson to his students as he lay dying.

Hearing that their teacher was about to die, Zusya's students came to pay him one last visit. On entering the room, they were surprised to see Zusya trembling with fear.

"Why are you afraid of death?" they asked. "Have you not been as righteous as Moses?"

Zusya answered, "When I stand before the throne of judgment, I won't be asked, 'Why were you not like Moses?' Rather, I'll be asked, 'Zusya, why were you not like Zusya?'"

What makes you *you*? Describe one of your best qualities—for example, kindness or truthfulness—that helps you add to the goodness of Creation. Describe an action that quality has helped you take—for example, tell how your kindness helped you cheer up a friend who was ill.

_____

_____

_____

_____

Think about specific qualities that you would like to strengthen in yourself. Then write a prayer asking for the willingness to strengthen those qualities in yourself.

_____

_____

_____

and planting gardens, so, too, do our souls enable us to feel compassion and kindness, to feel inspired to make the world a more just and peaceful place.

In fact, the human body and soul were formed to work together. For example, our souls teach us that it is right to give tzedakah and to act with lovingkindness, and our legs and arms do the work to feed hungry people at a soup kitchen. Our souls teach us that it is right to speak honestly, and our throats and lips form words of truth. How we act, not how we look, reflects that we are creatures made in God's image.

When our bodies and souls work together we can create magnificent art, such as this tapestry of Noah's ark by Lydie Egosi.

And because every human being is made of both the dust of the earth and a soul, our tradition teaches that every person—Jew and non-Jew alike—has great value and the potential to add to the goodness of Creation.

VALUE
Yourself

In a famous story from the Talmud, a man comes to the sage Hillel and tells him that he will convert to Judaism if Hillel can explain the Torah while standing on one foot. Hillel replied, "What is hateful to you do not do to any person. That is the whole Torah. All the rest is commentary." He then told the man, "Now, go and study the Torah."

The source of Hillel's wisdom is the commandment to "love your neighbor as yourself" (Leviticus 19:18). In other words, Judaism teaches that it's good to care about ourselves but that we must also show that same respect to others.

To develop self-respect, or self-esteem, we must treat ourselves with kindness and dignity and ask others to do the same. We treat ourselves well by taking good care of our bodies, being patient with ourselves when we make mistakes, and working to do our best in school.

But how can you tell the difference between behavior that develops self-esteem and behavior that is selfish?

Self-esteem motivates us to treat ourselves well; selfishness blinds us to the rights and needs of others. Self-esteem helps us respect our preferences and point of view; selfishness fools us into believing that what we want is the only thing that counts and what we think is the only thing that matters.

Bible Bio:
Pharaoh's Daughter

The Torah teaches that Miriam watched over her infant brother, Moses, as he lay in a basket on the Nile River. It then tells us how Pharaoh's daughter took compassion on him:

וַתֵּרֶא אֶת־הַתֵּבָה בְּתוֹךְ הַסּוּף וַתִּשְׁלַח אֶת־אֲמָתָהּ וַתִּקָּחֶהָ׃
וַתִּפְתַּח וַתִּרְאֵהוּ אֶת־הַיֶּלֶד וְהִנֵּה־נַעַר בֹּכֶה וַתַּחְמֹל עָלָיו
וַתֹּאמֶר מִיַּלְדֵי הָעִבְרִים זֶה׃

"[Pharaoh's daughter] spied the basket among the reeds and sent her maiden to fetch it. When she opened the basket, she saw the infant crying. She took pity on him and said, 'This must be an Israelite child.'" (Exodus 2:5–6)

Although her father had commanded that all Israelite sons be drowned in the Nile, Pharaoh's daughter rescued Moses and raised him as her son. The ancient rabbis honored her with the name Bityah, meaning "God's Daughter," because of her compassion for human life.

Henrietta Szold

Baltimore-born Henrietta Szold (1860–1945) was strong and determined. In 1909, she made her first visit to Palestine—which is what Israel was called before it became the modern Jewish state in 1948. Particularly troubled by the unhealthy living conditions of the children there, Szold returned to New York to form Hadassah, the Women's Zionist Organization of America. For the rest of her life, Szold worked to improve health care and education in the Land of Israel.

Haddassah Hospital opened in Jerusalem in 1925. Today it is considered one of the finest hospitals in the Middle East. It continues Henrietta Szold's commitment to caring for human life by providing quality medical care not only to Jews but also to thousands of Christians and Muslims within Israel and from neighboring Arab countries.

Self-esteem can help us express our opinions in class and our preference for how we want to spend our leisure time. It does not demand that others think as we do or that others make the same choices. But it can help us listen to those who disagree with us and to make compromises when necessary.

Sometimes it can be difficult to figure out whether an action is a sign of self-esteem or selfishness. Imagine that it's the night before your big social studies test. It's eight-thirty, and you've been told to be in bed by ten. You have exactly enough time to finish studying. Your friend calls, panicked because she needs help in Spanish. She asks you to spend an hour helping her. She lives next door and is prepared to come right over.

Would it be a sign of self-esteem or a sign of selfishness to study for your test instead of helping your friend? Would you be able to study for your test *and* help her? What might you say to her?

ME First?

Jewish tradition requires that we consider ourselves as we consider others. Sometimes we must even consider ourselves first. For

From the time we are little, our parents help us learn to take care of ourselves—to wear a hat and drink plenty of water when we're out in the heat and to wear a life jacket on a boat. They also teach us to be thoughtful of others and to share what we have. How might you have been different if your parents hadn't taught you these lessons?

Not only was Henrietta Szold deeply committed to the Land of Israel, but she also served the Jewish community in the United States, as a religious school teacher. How can you show commitment both to your Jewish community and to the Land of Israel?

example, in an aircraft emergency, parents are supposed to put on their own oxygen masks before putting on their children's masks. Why? Because if they don't, they may have difficulty breathing and be unable to help their kids. By following those instructions, parents not only obey the instructions of the airlines but also follow Judaism's teaching to do one's best to save a human life.

What about people who put their lives at risk by trying to rescue others? For example, firefighters put themselves in harm's way every day for the sake of others. Is that a Jewish way to behave?

Yes, it is. For firefighters are trained to save lives while minimizing the risk to themselves. It is their responsibility not only to help others but also to take the best possible care of themselves as they do. Similarly, if a person in a dangerous situation—for example, a shipwreck or a car accident—has reason to believe that he or she can save someone else's life, the commandment to "love your neighbor as yourself" requires that person to try to do so while caring for his or her own life as well.

Our tradition also teaches that if we know of others in need of food and shelter, we are required to help them. Yet we are not to give all our money to tzedakah in order to help others. For what purpose would it serve if, as a result, we, too, needed to receive tzedakah?

DO YOUR Best

Psalm 8:6 praises God for making humans in the image of God:

You have made humans just a bit less than divine,
And have crowned them with glory and honor.

Yet no matter how hard we try, we will never be perfect. No matter how hard we work to avoid selfishness, we sometimes have selfish impulses. And sometimes it's a close call: It can be difficult to know whether we must put our needs before those of others or whether it would be selfish to do so. Sometimes the best we can do is try to hear the still, small voice of our souls—the breath of God within us. That voice may encourage us to say, "No, I cannot help my friend because I need to study" or "Yes, I can help because I can rearrange my plans."

Your life, like the life of every person around you, is of infinite value—equal to the whole of Creation. By treating yourself with patience and respect, you can learn to love and value yourself and to treat others in the same way. It is the most important lesson Judaism has to teach. Now go and study Torah.

Sometimes when a parent's attention is focused on someone else—perhaps a brother or sister—we may become impatient or upset while waiting for our turn. At such times, how can we remember to balance our needs with those of others?

תְּחִי־נַפְשִׁי וּתְהַלְלֶךָּ
Let me live that I may praise You.
—Psalm 119:175

LEARN iT & LiVE iT

▶ **1.** Create a Ten Commandments of Loving Yourself to teach people to treat themselves with respect. For example, the first commandment might be "You shall eat healthy food."

1. You Shall _____

2. You Shall _____

3. You Shall _____

4. You Shall _____

5. You Shall _____

6. You Shall _____

7. You Shall _____

8. You Shall _____

9. You Shall _____

10. You Shall _____

Choose one of your commandments, and explain why you think it can help people develop self-respect.

_____

_____

▶ **2.** Describe one way in which you add goodness to your home.

_____

▶ **3.** Describe one way in which you add goodness to your school.

_____

צְאוּ וּרְאוּ אֵיזוֹהִי דֶרֶךְ יְשָׁרָה שֶׁיִּדְבַּק בָּה הָאָדָם...צְאוּ וּרְאוּ
אֵיזוֹהִי דֶרֶךְ רָעָה שֶׁיִּתְרַחֵק מִמֶּנָּה הָאָדָם:

Rabbi Yoḥanan taught, "Go forth and see which is the good way to which a person should hold. . . . Go forth and see which is the evil way which a person should avoid."
—*Pirkei Avot* 2:9

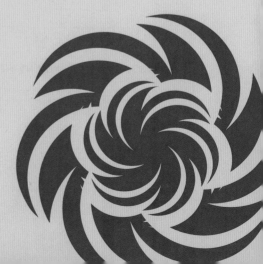

CHAPTER 3

THE VALUE OF
Free Will

Once a mischievous young boy noticed a sparrow nesting in a low bush. Quickly he grabbed the bird and walked over to his older sister. Holding the tiny bird behind his back, the boy said, "I have a sparrow in my hands. Tell me, is it dead or alive?"

Suspecting that her brother wanted to trick her, the girl reasoned that the bird must be alive. For if it was dead and she said so, there would be nothing her brother could do to prove her wrong. But if the bird was alive and she said so, he might crush it just to prove her wrong.

The girl wanted to spare the bird's life and help her brother understand that he was responsible for his actions. So when the boy repeated his question, "Is the bird dead or alive?" she replied, "I do not know, for the answer is in your hands."

—based on *Genesis Rabbah* 19:11

If you could have spoken to the young boy, what would you have said to help him make a good choice?

CHOICES AND
Impulses

The Torah teaches that God created light, heaven, and the earth first. Then God filled the earth with great rivers and blue oceans and with insects, plants, and animals of every sort. But of the hundreds of thousands of God's creations, only human beings were given free will—the ability to understand the difference between right and wrong—and the power to choose between the two.

The ancient rabbis taught that each time we are given a choice between good and bad, two impulses try to influence us. One is our desire to do what is good. That impulse is called *yetzer hatov*. The other impulse is our desire to do what is wrong. It is called *yetzer hara*.

When we're feeling grouchy and out of sorts and we can't switch our mood like the channels on our TV, it's best to wait before making an important decision. When we feel better, it is easier to pick up signals from the yetzer hatov.

POWER AND FREEDOM

Maimonides—a rabbi, doctor, scientist, and philosopher who lived in the twelfth century—taught, "Free will is given to every human being. If a person wants to turn toward the way of goodness and be righteous, that person has the power to do so. If a person wants to turn toward the way of evil and be wicked, that person has the freedom to do so" (*Mishneh Torah*).

In your opinion, why do people sometimes choose evil over good?

_____

_____

_____

_____

Know Right from Wrong

Judaism teaches that all God's creations—including animals and the natural environment—should be valued and treated with respect. But only humans are made in God's image, and only humans are given the ability to know right from wrong.

For example, a dog can be trained to sit quietly while the family is at the dinner table. But it cannot understand that it's rude to interrupt people when they are eating. Unlike human beings, a dog can't understand the difference between right and wrong no matter how much of an effort you make to explain it.

How would you train a dog to sit quietly while the family eats dinner?

_____

_____

_____

_____

How would you teach a young child that it is impolite to interrupt someone who is speaking?

_____

_____

_____

_____

Everyone is influenced by both the *yetzer hatov* and the *yetzer hara*. For example, someone may be influenced by the *yetzer hatov* to help an elderly person carry a heavy package or to visit a sick friend. That same person may be influenced by the *yetzer hara* to speak rudely to a stranger on line at a movie theater or to throw litter out a car window.

Think of a time when you felt a tug between the two impulses—the *yetzer hatov* and the *yetzer hara*—and chose to do good. Perhaps you were considering whether to do your homework or play video games or whether to pick a flower from someone's garden or just admire it. How did it feel to make the good choice? How did your choice influence the way you see yourself?

Now think of someone you admire and want to be like. In your view, how has that person been influenced by the *yetzer hatov*? What decisions might he or she have had to make that required listening to the *yetzer hatov*?

Sometimes we may not feel like listening to the *yetzer hatov*, but we listen anyway because we want to feel good about ourselves or because we know that it will help us achieve an important goal. So we pay attention to the quiet voice inside us that tells us to study for a test, help our

This child has been taught how to play with a dog safely and respectfully. But knowing what is right is not the same as doing it. So each time the boy plays with the dog, he must choose to do what he knows is right.

Bible Bio: Rebecca

Our patriarch Abraham sent his servant to Haran in search of a bride for his son Isaac. On arriving at a spring on the outskirts of the city, the servant ran to a young woman who had just drawn water from a well. He asked for a sip of water from her jar. Though she might have denied his request or given him only one sip, she let him drink his fill and watered his camels as well.

The young woman, whose name was Rebecca, responded to her *yetzer hatov* by choosing to be generous and caring:

וַתְּכַל לְהַשְׁקֹתוֹ וַתֹּאמֶר גַּם לִגְמַלֶּיךָ אֶשְׁאָב עַד אִם־כִּלּוּ לִשְׁתֹּת:

"When Rebecca had let the servant drink until he was satisfied, she said, 'I will also draw water for your camels, until they, too, have had their fill.'" (Genesis 24:19)

Rebecca was chosen as Isaac's wife and became a matriarch of the Jewish people.

mom, or go to our music lesson, and afterward we feel better for having done so.

The *yetzer hara* wields its greatest influence when we feel bad, when we're hurt, angry, or jealous. For example, if a parent seems more tolerant of a younger brother's mistakes, the *yetzer hara* may tempt us to tease our brother or play an unkind trick. It may seem as if being unkind to our sibling will make us feel better. It may even feel good the moment we do it. But does the good feeling from hurting someone last?

THE EXTRAORDINARY ACTS OF ORDINARY PEOPLE:
Lillian Wald

Lillian Wald (1867–1940) was born into a wealthy Jewish family in Cincinnati, Ohio. Though her wealth permitted her to choose a life of self-indulgence and luxury, Wald instead became a nurse and a peace activist, dedicating herself to relieving human suffering.

As the founder of the Visiting Nurse Service and the Henry Street Settlement, Wald provided important services to immigrants and the poor, including home health care and instruction in hygiene, parenting, English, and the arts. Wald fought for laws to protect the rights of women and children and was an active member of the Women's Peace Party.

Judaism teaches that all human beings are born good and given the gift of free will. How we use that gift is our choice.

The challenge to each of us is to overcome the impulse to do what we know is wrong and hurtful. The Talmud describes that impulse in three ways: At first, the *yetzer hara* is as light as a spider's web, but in the end it can become as heavy as thick ropes. At first, the *yetzer hara* is like a passerby, then like a guest, and finally it becomes the master of the house. At first, the *yetzer hara* is sweet, but in the end it is bitter.

How does the *yetzer hara* go from being light, unimportant, and sweet to heavy, powerful, and bitter? Perhaps in the beginning we think, "I'll give into it just this once," but then find that we give into it again and again until finally it becomes acceptable or even a habit. Perhaps it's that at first it feels good to get back at someone with whom we are angry or it feels good to avoid taking responsibility for our actions, but then we discover how bad it feels to lose the friendship or the respect of others.

So, how good do we have to be to prevent the *yetzer hara* from gaining control? Must we never give into it? Must we be perfect?

A BAD HABIT

"When a person commits a sin once and then a second time, . . . it appears to that person that it is no longer a sin." (Talmud, *Yoma* 86b)

Do you agree with the ancient rabbis that the more often we commit a wrong, the less wrong it seems to be? Why or why not? Before answering, think of examples, such as copying someone's homework or lying.

_____

_____

_____

_____

OOH, IT'S SO TEMPTING

"Opportunity knocks only once, but temptation leans on the doorbell" (Anonymous).

What helps you make good choices when temptation leans on the doorbell?

_____

_____

People Can Be Like Fire

Fire can nurture life through the warmth and light it provides. It can heat nourishing food, warm shivering bodies, and brighten darkened rooms. But it can also destroy. If a flame touches the edge of a curtain or the dry leaves on the forest floor, it can spread and destroy everything in its path.

People can be like fire. They can be a source of goodness and warmth or a source of destruction and hurt. But unlike fire, people have free will; they can make choices.

What might life be like if humans didn't have free will and therefore could do only good?

_____

_____

_____

_____

If you could, would you give up the gift of free will? Why or why not?

_____

_____

_____

_____

WE ARE IMPERFECT
but Good

In his book *How Good Do We Have to Be?* Rabbi Harold Kushner explains, "Life is not a spelling bee, where no matter how many words you have gotten right, if you make one mistake you are disqualified. Life is more like a baseball season, where even the best team loses one-third of its games. . . . Our goal is to win more than we lose, and if we can do that consistently enough, then when the end comes, we will have won it all."

The Torah teaches that even the greatest heroes of the Bible—among them Noah, Sarah, Jacob, and Moses—made mistakes. Noah got drunk, Sarah was unkind to Hagar, Jacob tricked his brother and lied to his father, and Moses ignored God's instructions on how to bring forth water from a rock. How is it possible that the Torah's models of goodness are imperfect?

Think about it. How might you react if you were asked to model yourself on someone who had never made a mistake, someone who was perfect—doing everything right, from scoring straight A's to never speaking a harsh word, never losing a tennis match, winning every science-fair competition and essay contest?

At first glance, this might look like a piece of art—a statue—but in fact it's a living person. However, there is an art to being a person; it is in doing one's best to live as a creature made in the image of God.

36

Come Down to Earth

The Ḥasidic rabbi Moshe of Kobryn once looked up toward the sky and cried: "Dear angel! It is no trick to be an angel in heaven. You don't have to eat and drink, and earn money. Come down to earth and worry about these things, and we shall see if you remain an angel." (Martin Buber, *Tales of Hasidism*)

Write a short script or story about an angel who visits earth for a day and discovers how challenging it is to be a boy or girl your age.

_____

_____

_____

_____

_____

_____

_____

_____

ANGEL OR SAINT?

Albert Schweitzer (1875–1965) worked in what is now Gabon, Africa, as a doctor and Christian missionary for over forty years. In honor of his lifetime of humanitarian service, including providing medical aid to those suffering from leprosy, Schweitzer won the Nobel Peace Prize in 1952. It was Schweitzer's belief that "you don't have to be an angel in order to be a saint." What do you think he meant?

_____

_____

_____

How can remembering Albert Schweitzer's words help you continue to work at becoming your best self after you've made a mistake or fallen short of your mark?

_____

_____

_____

Our tradition teaches that no one is perfect but everyone can be wonderful. After all, despite their flaws, Noah was a righteous man who followed in God's holy ways of mercy and justice, Sarah was a courageous woman who went forth with Abraham to give birth to the Jewish people, Jacob struggled with his conscience, and Moses led the Israelites out of slavery and became the greatest prophet the Jewish people have ever had.

In fact, rather than being disappointed by our ancestors' imperfections, we are inspired by their lives. For it is precisely because they were imperfect yet good that we know we, too, are capable of much goodness despite our flaws.

A scribe is highly trained to do the sacred work of writing and repairing Torah scrolls. Like other people, much as scribes try to work carefully, they sometimes make mistakes. When they do, all that is required is that they correct the error.

A MINYAN OF THIEVES?

"Ten people join together to steal a beam, and are not ashamed in each other's presence." (Talmud, *Kiddushin* 80b)

In your own words, explain what lesson the sages wanted to teach with that example.

_____

_____

_____

_____

WE ARE RESPONSIBLE FOR
Our Choices

Have you ever done something you knew was wrong, felt a twinge of guilt, but told yourself, "No big deal—everyone does it"? Perhaps rather than do your homework, you copied a friend's, or maybe you gossiped about or teased a classmate.

Can we decide that doing something wrong is not so bad when lots of other people do it too? Does accepting that you are human—imperfect—mean that you don't have to try to become your best self?

Our tradition teaches that because we have free will, we are each responsible for our choices no matter what other people do. It tells us that we must strive to right our own wrongs and to become our best selves.

That is why on Rosh Hashanah and Yom Kippur we look back on the previous year to acknowledge both our achievements and our mistakes. That is why each year on those holy days we begin—though we never complete—the work of self-improvement. And that is why even though we may want to say, "I'm not responsible" or "They started it" or "It's not my fault!" we instead say, "I'm sorry; please forgive me. Can I make it up to you?" No matter what others do, we are responsible for our own actions.

Any time can be a good time to work toward self-improvement. In the middle of the year, in the middle of the street, you may imagine that you hear the wake-up call of the shofar, or ram's horn, asking you to think about the choices you've made, the ones you're proud of and the ones you would like to improve on.

We Don't Only Wrong Others

Sometimes we wrong ourselves. We wrong ourselves, for example, when we ride a scooter without wearing a helmet, when we let our fear of failure discourage us from accepting challenging tasks, or when we give in to peer pressure even though we don't agree with our friends.

Have you wronged yourself in any way this week? How can you develop the willingness to both forgive yourself and try to do better in the future?

_____

_____

_____

_____

How has the yetzer hatov influenced you to take good care of yourself this week?

Ancient Stories for Modern Times

THEY DID IT FIRST!

One day while hurrying on his way, Rabbi Joshua ben Ḥananyah noticed a wheat field with a shortcut, a path that had been worn by other travelers. He began to cross the field when he saw a young girl. "Where do you think you're going?" she called to him. "This is my father's field."

"I am only following a path that is already made," the rabbi answered.

"Yes," she responded, "but the path was made by others like you who have already harmed the crops. Will you follow in their footsteps to do evil?" (based on Talmud, *Eruvin* 53b)

Summarize the lesson of this story.

_____

_____

_____

In the story, a rabbi is taught by a child. What might the rabbis of the Talmud want us to learn from this?

_____

_____

_____

STUDY HELPS US
Make Good Choices

To help strengthen the influence of our *yetzer hatov*, our impulse to do good, Jewish tradition teaches us to study Torah. For Torah teaches what is good and how to take responsibility for our actions. The stories and laws of the Torah teach us how to learn from the goodness of others and how to recognize when others are leading us astray.

Learning to choose fair, kind, and responsible actions can help you select the friends, leisure activities, and work that will become a source of satisfaction and dignity. And learning how to forgive yourself when you make mistakes can help you accept the challenge of becoming the best person you can be.

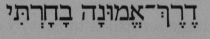

דֶּרֶךְ־אֱמוּנָה בָחָרְתִּי

I have chosen the way of faith.
—Psalm 119:30

LEARN iT & LiVE iT

▶ **1.** Do you think that free will is like a driver's license—that one should be at least a teenager and pass a test before receiving it? Why or why not?

_____

_____

▶ **2.** How might making good choices help you become not only a better person but also a happier one?

_____

_____

▶ **3.** Describe a good choice that is difficult for you to make—for example, offering to help with household chores or speaking to others honestly yet respectfully when you feel hurt or angry.

_____

_____

What small step can you take to help make that choice more often than you do now?

_____

_____

▶ **4.** In the space below, draw an illustration of the *yetzer hatov* and the *yetzer hara* trying to influence you.

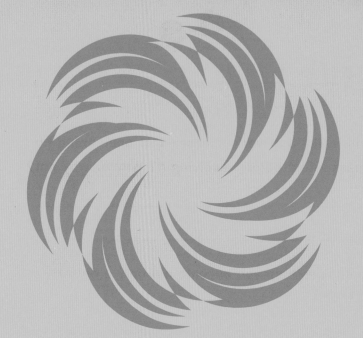

לֹא עָלֶיךָ הַמְּלָאכָה לִגְמוֹר וְלֹא אַתָּה בֶן חוֹרִין לִבָּטֵל מִמֶּנָּה׃

Rabbi Tarfon taught, "It is not your duty to complete the work; neither are you free to stop persisting."

—*Pirkei Avot* 2:16

CHAPTER 4

THE VALUE OF Persistence

Two years after their liberation from Pharaoh's Egypt, the Israelites had not yet reached the Promised Land. Exhausted and impatient, they continued on their journey through the Sinai Desert. But slowly they began to wonder whether life in Egypt had really been so bad. True, the Land of Israel was promised to them by God, but the challenge of their journey was proving greater than they had imagined.

Frustrated, the Israelites began to complain: "If only we had meat to eat! We remember the free fish, . . . the cucumbers, the melons, the leeks, the onions, and the garlic. But now our lives are dry. There is nothing at all! Nothing but this manna to look forward to. . . . Oh, why did we ever leave Egypt!"

—Numbers 11

• ❈ •

This story reminds us that when our goals are ambitious, it may take us a long time to succeed. We may experience disappointments and even the loss of faith. But just as the Israelites persisted and eventually reached the Promised Land, so, too, can we persist and accomplish our own goals in the process.

JUST KEEP ON
Keepin' On

Think about a time when you worked hard to achieve a goal but succeeded only after many tries. For example, you might have suffered through a hundred exasperating (and painful!) belly flops before learning to dive, or you might have practiced a song on the piano or guitar for weeks before getting it right. Perhaps you studied a new prayer in Hebrew, reading it aloud over and over, stumbling over certain words time and again before you could pronounce them correctly.

How did you feel as you kept trying? Did you want to give up at some point? What helped you continue until you succeeded? How did you feel when you finally got it right? Was it worth the effort?

One of the greatest challenges for each of us is to do our best. As Jews, that requires us to do our part to fulfill the *Brit*, our people's Covenant with God. For example, each of us must try our best to help feed and clothe those in need, visit the sick, and show compassion for animals. However, neither must we achieve these goals all at once, nor must we work at them by ourselves.

Do you remember the first time you recited the Four Questions at the Passover seder? How long did you practice before you got them right?

ONE LIFE,
Many Opportunities

Sometimes as we're working toward a goal, we may become frustrated or even lose faith that we can overcome the obstacles or challenges before us. At such times, it's useful to remember that within a person's lifetime, there are many opportunities to grow and succeed. Rabbi Yehudah ben

Teimah taught that in every life there are phases, or seasons, each with its own purpose and strength:

> **At five years, the age is reached for studying the Bible,**
> **At ten, for the study of Mishnah,**
> **At thirteen, for doing the *mitzvot*,**
> **At fifteen, for the study of Talmud,**
> **At eighteen, for marriage,**
> **At twenty, for seeking a livelihood,**
> **At thirty, for entering into one's full strength,**
> **At forty, for understanding,**
> **At fifty, for wise advice,**
> **At sixty, for attaining old age,**
> **At seventy, for the silver head,**
> **At eighty, the gift of special strength.**
>
> **—*Pirkei Avot* 5:21**

In the centuries that have passed since the wisdom of Yehudah ben Teimah was recorded, some things have changed (you probably won't get married when you're eighteen), and some have remained the same (you, too, will probably explore career possibilities and studies when you're twenty). Most important, as *Pirkei Avot* teaches, each age brings new challenges and new strengths.

When you feel frustrated because you're not able to move ahead as quickly as you would like, try listing all you've learned since you entered first grade: how to read books in English and prayers in Hebrew, prepare a

Sometimes we may be in a big rush. We may wonder why it takes us so long to learn what we need to know and do. But different people have different skills and abilities; each of us learns some things quickly, while other things take us more time.

meal for yourself, tell time, solve math problems, teach others to solve math problems, recite the blessings over the Ḥanukkah candles, play a musical instrument or a team sport, comfort someone who is sad, and at least one thousand other things.

Then imagine all you will have learned by the time you enter high school or college or by the time you start your first job. And then try to imagine what it would have been like if after stumbling over the first words you read in kindergarten, you had given up and decided that you would never learn to read. How many books would you have missed out on? How many subjects would you have been unable to study? How many friends could you not have e-mailed? And how many street and road signs could you not have made sense of?

So it is with persisting as a member of the Covenant. If our ancestors had stopped trying to succeed every time they faced obstacles that are not

Bible Bio: Moses

Moses was chosen by God to lead the Israelites out of slavery in ancient Egypt so that they could become a free people who served God. Pharaoh repeatedly refused to let the Israelites go, but Moses persisted in his efforts. Though he was not confident that he could meet the challenge God had set before him, Moses continued to follow God's instructions, no matter how many times he failed to persuade Pharaoh to let the Israelites leave Egypt.

The Bible teaches that when God told Moses, "I will send you to Pharaoh, and you shall free My people, the Israelites, from Egypt," Moses humbly responded:

מִי אָנֹכִי כִּי אֵלֵךְ אֶל־פַּרְעֹה וְכִי אוֹצִיא אֶת־בְּנֵי יִשְׂרָאֵל מִמִּצְרָיִם:

"Who am I that I should go to Pharaoh and free the Israelites from Egypt?" (Exodus 3:11)

Yet through faith and persistence, and with the help of his brother, Aaron, Moses succeeded.

Moses succeeded in leading the Israelites out of Egypt with the help of his brother. What difficult task have you accomplished with the help of a family member or friend?

easy to overcome, they would have given up the goal of living in freedom, and the Jewish people might still be enslaved or wandering through the Sinai Desert.

The Israelites chose not to give up even when they felt disheartened, and we, too, may need to keep trying even when we feel impatient or begin to lose faith. But just as our ancestors worked together and succeeded in doing much good, so can we.

We may not be able to stop a war in a foreign country, but we can stop yelling at those we love. We may not be able to feed every hungry person in the world, but we can do our part by setting aside some of our money for tzedakah.

THE EXTRAORDINARY ACTS OF ORDINARY PEOPLE:
Natan Sharansky

Natan Sharansky was born in 1948 in the former Soviet Union. In 1977, he was charged with spying for the United States and imprisoned by the Communist government. However, the real reason for his arrest was his effort to help other Soviet Jews who—like him—had been refused the right to immigrate to Israel.

In his autobiography *Fear No Evil*, Natan Sharansky explained that while the Communist system tried to enslave him, Jewish tradition helped him find the courage to persist in his fight for freedom, truth, and justice. After nine years of imprisonment, Sharansky was permitted to immigrate to Israel. He has held several ministerial positions in the Israeli government, including minister of industry and trade (1996–1999) and minister of the interior (1999–2000).

And we may not be able to force others to conserve natural resources, but we can recycle paper and turn off the lights we are not using.

If we are patient and persist in our efforts, as we grow older we will meet goals that might have felt impossible to achieve when we were younger. We can learn to do our part and to work with others—friends, family, and members of our synagogue and our secular community. Working with others, we can raise money to help feed many people, build many schools and hospitals in poor countries, and influence politicians to work for peace and care for the environment.

A JOB FOR
Many Generations

But even though we persist and try our best, our sages recognized that the task of making the world a better place cannot be completed by one person, one community, or even one generation.

Have you ever felt like a lucky dog because you achieved something without really trying? How often does that happen? Are you willing to rely on luck to help you accomplish what you want? Why or why not?

IT'S MY GOAL

List two goals that you think are important for you to achieve within the next two years.

1._____

2._____

Which of those goals would require that you work hard? Write the number(s) of the goal(s).

_____

Will it be worth the effort? Why or why not?

_____

_____

_____

_____

_____

Sometimes a challenge may seem too great—like climbing a great mountain or a steep rock formation. But with patience and persistence, we can develop the skills to succeed.

to the next generation, hoping and trusting that some day the work will be completed.

The Israelites wandered through the Sinai Desert for forty years before they reached the Promised Land. Along the way, they suffered many failures and frustrations, and leadership was passed from Moses to Joshua. The generation that had fled Egypt died before reaching the

At the close of Shabbat, during the havdalah ceremony, we inhale the fragrant scent from a spice, or b'sumim, box. This strengthens us as we leave the peace and beauty of Shabbat and return to the hustle and bustle of the work week. What personal ritual or ceremony might you create to help strengthen yourself when it's difficult for you to persist in your goals?

Let Us Begin

On January 20, 1961, in his inaugural address, John F. Kennedy spoke with passion about all nations working together to spread liberty and justice throughout the world. He understood that the task was great and would be completed not by one generation but through the efforts of many. He said, "All this will not be finished . . . in the life of this administration, nor even perhaps in our lifetime on this planet. But let us begin."

President Kennedy's speech echoed the teaching of the ancient sage Rabbi Tarfon, whose words opened this chapter: "It is not your duty to complete the work; neither are you free to stop persisting."

In your own words, explain the lessons of these wise leaders.

_____

_____

_____

_____

Ancient Stories for Modern Times

THE CAROB TREE

The sage Rabbi Yoḥanan tells the story of a righteous man named Onias, also known as Ḥoni, who learned how each generation gives to the next.

One day while walking along the road, Ḥoni saw a man planting a carob tree and said to him, "Since a carob tree does not bear fruit for seventy years, are you certain of living so long as to eat the fruit of the tree you are planting?"

The man replied, "I found the world filled with carob trees because my ancestors planted them for me. I am planting them now for my children." (Talmud, *Ta'anit* 23a)

Name two things that you can enjoy because your parents or grandparents or other members of your community worked to provide you with them—for example, your home or a local park or playground.

1. _____

2. _____

Name two things that you would like to help provide for the next generation.

1. _____

2. _____

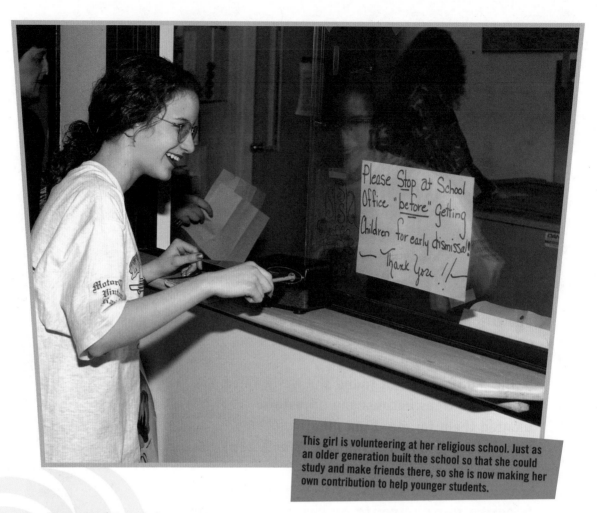

This girl is volunteering at her religious school. Just as an older generation built the school so that she could study and make friends there, so she is now making her own contribution to help younger students.

Promised Land, but a new generation grew up and accepted the challenge of doing their part to fulfill the *Brit*.

It is many generations later, and our people now live all around the world, as far away as Australia and Israel. Yet we still share the dream of a more peaceful and a more just world, and we continue to do our part—comforting one another when we fail and celebrating when we succeed. And we will continue to do our part until it is time to pass on our dream to the next generation.

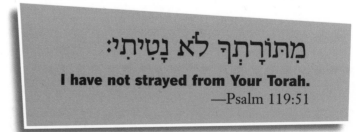

מִתּוֹרָתְךָ לֹא נָטִיתִי:
I have not strayed from Your Torah.
—Psalm 119:51

LEARN iT & LiVE iT

▶ **1.** Describe a skill that you would like to develop or improve. For example, you might want to learn how to play a musical instrument or improve your tennis serve.

_____

_____

How can being patient with yourself help you persist?

_____

▶ **2.** Describe two ways in which you can help make the world a better place for the next generation.

A. _____

_____

B. _____

_____

How can working with others in your religious school or synagogue help you succeed?

_____

How might your religious school studies help you succeed?

_____

_____

▶ **3.** How can you encourage yourself to persist when you miss the mark? For example, do you have a hero whose persistence can inspire you?

_____

_____

_____

הֲפֹךְ בָּהּ וַהֲפֹךְ בָּהּ, דְּכֹלָּא בָהּ; וּבַהּ תֶּחֱזֵי...וּמִנַּהּ לָא תָזוּעַ
שֶׁאֵין לָךְ מִדָּה טוֹבָה הֵימֶנָּה:

Ben Bag-Bag taught, "Turn it [the Torah] again and again, for everything is in it; think about it . . . and do not stray from it, for there is no greater good."

—*Pirkei Avot 5:22*

CHAPTER 5

THE VALUE OF
Study

An ancient legend teaches that when our ancestors stood at Mount Sinai, God said to them, "Before I give you My Torah, you must give me something precious that proves you will be devoted to it."

The Israelites thought long and hard. They offered their jewelry. But God did not accept it. Then they thought harder about what was most precious and offered the patriarchs and matriarchs—Abraham and Sarah, Isaac and Rebecca, and Jacob, Rachel, and Leah—as proof. But God refused that offer too.

Finally the Israelites said, "Our children and all generations of children after them are what is most precious. We will teach them to love and honor God's commandments."

Pleased, God responded, "For their sake, I will give you the Torah."

—Song of Songs Rabbah

Imagine receiving a board game without instructions. It might be a great game, but without the directions how could you play it?

In that same way, if we did not have the Torah, how would we know the ways in which we can serve God? the importance of seeking peace in our homes and justice on the playground? of being honest with our friends and compassionate to strangers? of treating ourselves and others with kindness and respect?

INSTRUCTIONS, Please!

One way to understand the importance of the Torah is to think of it as the Jewish book of instructions that comes with the gift of free will. In fact, one meaning of the word *torah* is "instruction."

Yes, there are other religions that teach many of the same values that Judaism teaches. But those religions can only provide the instructions on how to fulfill their religion's purpose. They cannot teach us how to fulfill the Jewish people's Covenant with God. For that, we need the Torah, the wisdom of our sages, and the willingness to add our own understanding and actions to the traditions of our people.

"Interesting," you may say, "but we live in a world that is very different from our ancestors' world. How can the Torah's instructions and the teachings of the sages be useful to us today?"

The telephone is a wonderful invention, but if we don't know how to make a call, it's not very useful. Similarly, free will can open a world of opportunities, but if we don't know how to make good choices, we can't benefit from it.

The World's First Torah in Outer Space

On March 2, 1996, Jeffrey A. Hoffman observed Shabbat by reading from the Book of Genesis. Why was that extraordinary? Hoffman read from a Torah scroll while orbiting above Jerusalem, aboard the space shuttle *Columbia*.

Hoffman explained why he chose to take a Torah scroll with him: "Wherever Jews have wandered, they have taken the Torah with them. Unlike other objects which become special by being in space, the Torah's holy status remains constant. What changes is the realization that the values and traditions that we carry with us will affect the human presence in space."

Because a standard Torah scroll is quite large, a special, much smaller scroll was taken on the mission so that it could be placed with Hoffman's personal belongings. The scroll, which is now housed in Hoffman's synagogue, Congregation Or Hadash in Houston, is seven inches long and four inches in diameter. It includes all five books of the Torah in Hebrew and was written by a trained scribe.

Ancient Stories for Modern Times

KINDERGARTEN AT AGE FORTY

Our tradition teaches that it's never too late to begin the study of Torah. The following legend tells about a man who began his studies at age forty.

There was a poor shepherd in ancient Israel who did not know how to read or write. When he was forty, his wife urged him to go to Jerusalem to study Torah. "But people will laugh at me, for I do not even know the *alef bet*," the man said.

"Bring me a donkey whose back is injured," answered the wife. Although he thought that an odd request, the shepherd did as his wife requested.

The wife covered the donkey's back with earth and herbs so that it looked ridiculous. The first day they took the donkey to market, everyone pointed at it and laughed. The second day, fewer people laughed. And by the third day, no one paid any attention to it.

"Go to Jerusalem, and study Torah," said the wife to her husband. "The first few days people may laugh, but by the end of the week you will be accepted for who you are."

The shepherd began studying with children in kindergarten, and once he started studying, he never stopped. That shepherd became one of the greatest sages of Israel, Rabbi Akiva.

How can a computer help you reach out to people in need?

It's true that we live in a world that is centuries removed from the experiences of our ancestors. Theirs was a world of quill pens and parchment. Ours is a world of keyboards and computer chips, a world in which information can be sent from one continent to another in seconds with a fax or on the beam of a satellite. But like the generations before us, by studying our sacred texts and traditions, we can learn to use the talents and tools of our time to help fulfill the *Brit* and make the world a better place.

Think about it: How can you use a telephone to fulfill the ancient mitzvah of visiting the sick, *bikur ḥolim*? What household tools can help you perform the Torah's instruction to honor parents, *kibud av va'eim*? A dishwasher? A vacuum cleaner? Or an old-fashioned broom? With the help of what technologies can you use your special talents to assist others?

What mitzvot can an old-fashioned bike help you fulfill?

READ! STUDY!
Action!

The most famous portion of the Torah, the one with which people around the world—Jews and non-Jews alike—are most familiar, is the Ten Commandments. Read the commandments, and try to figure out what they all have in common:

1. I am Adonai your God, who brought you out of the Land of Egypt.
2. Do not worship any other gods or any idols.
3. Do not swear falsely by the name of Adonai, your God.
4. Remember Shabbat, and keep it holy.
5. Honor your father and mother.
6. Do not murder.
7. Do not take another person's wife or husband.
8. Do not steal.
9. Do not tell lies about another person.
10. Do not desire what belongs to your neighbor.

All the commandments teach us the importance of actions. The first commandment sets the stage by stating the action God took so that we can serve God. The nine commandments that follow tell us how we can serve God, the actions we should and should not take.

As the Ten Commandments teach us the importance of our actions, so, too, does the Talmud. It teaches us that when a person dies, the first three questions he or she is asked in the heavenly court are these:

1. **Were you honest in your business dealings?**
2. **Did you regularly set time aside to study Torah?**
3. **Did you work at raising children?**

Knowing that our lives are judged according to our actions, what additional question might you add to the list?

Which of the Ten Commandments do you think is the easiest to obey? Why? Which do you think is the most difficult? Why?

THE GIFT THAT KEEPS
on Giving

Do you remember your favorite storybooks from when you were younger and the many times you asked your mom or dad to read them to you? Why did you like to hear those stories over and over again?

We dress Torah scrolls in decorative mantels, adorn them in silver, and carry them with great care.

Do you think that the same books you enjoy now will give you pleasure ten years from now? twenty or thirty years from now? Why or why not?

The Torah includes many wonderful stories that we can enjoy and learn from as young children, but which we never outgrow. We read them in synagogue each week —when we are young, when we are grown up, and when we are old. The older we become and the more times we read the Torah, the more we can learn from it. It is the gift that keeps on giving.

FROM START TO FINISH TO START

Each Shabbat we read the weekly portion of the Torah—called the *sidrah* or *parashah*—in synagogue. It takes exactly one year for us to complete our reading of the Torah. And as soon as we have finished, on the holiday of Simḥat Torah, we roll the scroll back to the beginning and start reading again.

OLDER AND WISER

It's wonderful to know that you can start learning something when you are young and deepen your pleasure as you grow older.

For example, if you play a sport such as tennis, golf, or basketball your understanding of the game probably grows with each year that you play, along with your pleasure and skills. At age six, you might have felt proud of your accomplishments, but by age seven you wanted to be able to do the same things—serve, swing, or dribble—only better. And with each year since then, your skills, understanding, and appreciation have undoubtedly grown.

Describe something you started to learn when you were young, and list two ways in which you have increased your understanding and your abilities as you've grown older.

_____

_____

1._____

2._____

Describe two things you know about the Torah now that you didn't know when you began religious school.

1.

_____

2.

_____

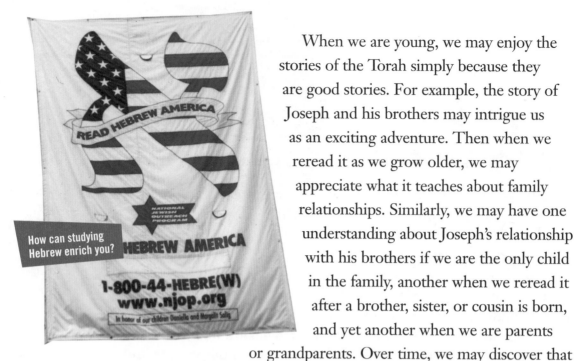

How can studying Hebrew enrich you?

READ HEBREW AMERICA

NATIONAL JEWISH OUTREACH PROGRAM

HEBREW AMERICA

1-800-44-HEBRE(W)
www.njop.org

In honor of our children Daniella and Margalit Selig

When we are young, we may enjoy the stories of the Torah simply because they are good stories. For example, the story of Joseph and his brothers may intrigue us as an exciting adventure. Then when we reread it as we grow older, we may appreciate what it teaches about family relationships. Similarly, we may have one understanding about Joseph's relationship with his brothers if we are the only child in the family, another when we reread it after a brother, sister, or cousin is born, and yet another when we are parents or grandparents. Over time, we may discover that the story helps us understand something about relationships in our own families and also about the love that binds us.

Talmud Torah—studying the Torah—helps us discover new details. Our rabbi or teacher may point out something we hadn't seen before—for example, that the story of Creation is told twice in the Book of Genesis, once in the first chapter and again in a slightly different way in the second. By rereading the stories, we may notice details that help us understand the value of the different versions. And with every new detail we notice, we may discover new lessons that help us become our best selves.

These mezuzah cases are different sizes, shapes, and colors, but the same scroll is inside each one. It reminds us of our Covenant with God and our duty to study and teach Torah.

Creation 1 and 2

In the first chapter of Genesis, we are taught: "And God created the human being in God's image, in the image of God the human being was created; male and female God created them" (1:27).

In the second chapter of Genesis, the creation of human beings is taught in this way: "Adonai created the human being [Adam] from the dust of the earth, and breathed the breath of life into the human's nostrils; and the human became a living soul" (2:7).

וַיִּיצֶר יְהוָה אֱלֹהִים אֶת־הָאָדָם עָפָר מִן־הָאֲדָמָה וַיִּפַּח בְּאַפָּיו נִשְׁמַת חַיִּים וַיְהִי הָאָדָם לְנֶפֶשׁ חַיָּה:

List two lessons that those verses teach us. Hint: See page 20.

_____

_____

_____

_____

Throughout the Day

The V'ahavta, which we recite as part of every prayer service, is included in the text inscribed on the small scroll inside a mezuzah case. It reminds us of our duty to grow continually in our understanding of Torah by thinking, teaching, and speaking words of Torah throughout each day.

"Take to heart these instructions, which I command you this day. Teach them to your children, and speak of them when you are at home and when you go on your way and when you lie down and when you get up." (Deuteronomy 6:6–7)

In your own words, write the meaning of the above verses from the V'ahavta.

_____

_____

_____

_____

In Israel, a mezuzah can be found on the doorpost of almost all buildings—movie theaters, cafes, schools, supermarkets, and banks.

WE NEED TO
Study to Survive

At synagogue services, each time we return the Torah scroll to the Ark, we sing, "The Torah is a tree of life to those who hold on to it." What do you think that means?

Torah study allows one generation to pass on Jewish wisdom and traditions to the next generation. It reminds us of Abraham and Sarah's courage to worship one God instead of bowing to idols, and of the Israelites' persistence in forging through the wilderness to the Promised Land. It deepens our knowledge of the *mitzvot* and enriches our dream of making a better world.

Because they knew that our people need Torah study to survive as Jews, the sages ruled almost two thousand years ago that parents of young children may not live in a city without schools and that the poor may not be charged for their education. Our sages also taught, "Say not, 'When I have leisure, I will study.' Perhaps you will have no leisure" (*Pirkei Avot* 2:5).

LIKE A FISH OUT OF WATER

Rabbi Akiva lived in the Land of Israel when the Romans ruled it. Although the Romans forbade the study of Torah, Akiva continued his studies. When asked why he was willing to risk his life for the sake of studying Torah, he explained, "Just as fish need water to live, so the Jewish people need Torah. Though it may be dangerous to continue studying, it would be far more dangerous to stop." And with that, the rabbi smiled and returned to his study of Torah. (Talmud, *B'rachot* 61b)

What do you think Rabbi Akiva meant when he said that it would be dangerous for our people to stop studying Torah?

_____

_____

_____

Do you agree or disagree with Akiva? Why or why not?

_____

_____

_____

_____

Bible Bio: The Israelites

The ancient Israelites were a diverse group. They included young and old people; short and tall people; people from different tribes, such as the tribes of Shimon, Levi, and Yehudah; and people who worked at different crafts and trades—potters, builders, shepherds, weavers, and healers. Our tradition teaches that despite their differences, all Israelites received the Torah, and no part of it was kept from any of them.

וַיְצַוֵּם אֵת כָּל־אֲשֶׁר דִּבֶּר יהוה אִתּוֹ בְּהַר סִינָי:

"And [Moses] instructed the Israelites concerning all that Adonai had said to him on Mount Sinai." (Exodus 34:32)

THE EXTRAORDINARY ACTS OF ORDINARY PEOPLE:
Rebecca Gratz

Rebecca Gratz (1781–1869) dedicated her life to helping others. She raised money for those in need and founded the Jewish Foster Home and Orphan Asylum. Gratz was also concerned about the religious education of Jewish children. In 1818, she founded the Hebrew Sunday School Society of Philadelphia.

That school was very different from other Jewish religious schools of its time. In the Hebrew Sunday School, boys and girls were taught together, classes were held only once a week, lessons were presented in English rather than Hebrew, and all of the teachers and administrators were women. The model quickly spread to other Jewish communities and has strongly influenced the development of modern Jewish education.

It is because of you, your classmates, and Jewish children around the world who study the values and traditions of our people that our ancestors were given the Torah. And it is because you and your generation do not wait until you have leisure time to study Torah—but instead come to religious school even when you feel tired or might prefer to play sports or video games—that the Jewish people will live on for many more generations, studying Torah and working to make a better world.

לַמְּדֵנִי חֻקֶּיךָ:

Teach me Your laws.
—Psalm 119:12

LEARN iT & LiVE iT

 1. Why do you think our tradition teaches that not only rabbis but *all* Jews must study Torah?

_____

_____

_____

_____

2. One of the best ways to learn is to teach, and one of the greatests acts of *talmud Torah* is to share the joy of learning with someone else. Describe a way in which you can teach others.

_____

_____

_____

3. In this space or on a separate piece of drawing paper, create a scene that illustrates these words: "The Torah is a tree of life to those who hold on to it."

אַל תִּפְרוֹשׁ מִן הַצִּבּוּר:

Hillel said, "Do not separate yourself from the community."
—*Pirkei Avot* 2:4

THE VALUE OF
Community

A Jewish folktale tells of a woman who visited a magnificent mansion. As she entered its great dining hall, to her amazement people were seated at an elegant table overflowing with food and drink, but no one was eating or drinking. Instead, all were wailing. Curious, the woman looked more closely and saw that the people could not bend their elbows and therefore could not bring the food or drink to their mouths.

Suddenly the woman heard sounds of merriment coming from an adjoining room. She peered into the second room, where she also saw people seated around a beautiful table piled high with savory food and drink. They, too, could not bend their elbows. But *they* rejoiced, for each person was serving his or her neighbor.

• • • • • • • • • • • • • 🌀 • • • • • • • • • • • • • •

What might your life be like if you had to do everything for yourself, with no help from anyone? Imagine that you had to grow your own food, make your own clothes, build your own house, and invent your own television and car. What if there was no one with whom to play in an orchestra or on a soccer team? no one with whom to celebrate your birthday or bat or bar mitzvah? no one with whom to eat latkes and applesauce?

BUILD A HOLY
Community

A group of people who live, work, study, pray, or play together may be called a community. And every community has a purpose. For example, the purpose of a medical community, such as the one formed by those who work in a hospital, is to help people recover from illness or injury or avoid becoming sick. The purpose of an educational community, such as a school, is to help students develop their values, skills, and abilities.

Most of us are members of several communities—for example, a family, a school, a sports team, and a synagogue. To what communities do you belong? What purpose does each have?

We live in a multicultural society, where several traditions may be found in a single community. For example, this New Orleans restaurant provides a taste of the south (Dixie), Greece (gyro), and the Jewish homeland—Israel (falafel)! Can you find the Hebrew word for falafel in the window?

Bible Bio: Jethro

Jethro was the priest of Midian and Moses' father-in-law. He understood that to be most effective, a great leader must reach out to members of the community for support and help. Therefore, when Moses tried to judge all legal arguments among the Israelites single-handedly, Jethro offered him wise counsel:

לֹא־תוּכַל עֲשֹׂהוּ לְבַדֶּךָ.... וְאַתָּה תֶחֱזֶה מִכָּל־הָעָם אַנְשֵׁי־חַיִל
יִרְאֵי אֱלֹהִים אַנְשֵׁי אֱמֶת.... וְהָיָה כָּל־הַדָּבָר הַגָּדֹל יָבִיאוּ אֵלֶיךָ
וְכָל־הַדָּבָר הַקָּטֹן יִשְׁפְּטוּ־הֵם....

"You cannot do it alone. . . . Seek out from among all the Israelites capable people who are filled with an awe of God and are trustworthy. . . . Have them bring every major dispute to you, but let them decide every minor dispute among themselves." (Exodus 18:18–22)

We Need One Another

Our lives are so complex that each of us needs the help of many other people, each with different talents and skills—doctors, teachers, farmers, plumbers, librarians, bakers, scientists, rabbis, and singers.

List six people by name, relationship, or profession whose help contributes to the goodness in your life.

1. _____
2. _____
3. _____
4. _____
5. _____
6. _____

Now list two people whom you have helped, and explain what you did.

1. _____
   _____
   _____
2. _____
   _____

The Jewish community has a very important purpose: to honor the Covenant, or *Brit*. We honor the *Brit* by living as a holy people—observing Shabbat and holidays and helping to bring more justice, mercy, and peace to the world. *Pirkei Avot* teaches that this tradition of Torah was passed down from God to Moses, from Moses to Joshua, from Joshua to the elders, from the elders to the prophets, from the prophets to the sages, and through the sages to us. Each of us is responsible for doing our part, for no one person—not even a whole generation—can fulfill the *Brit* alone.

To help themselves succeed, Jews come together to build a holy community—we study Torah, pray, celebrate, and offer help and comfort to those in need.

WE STUDY AS A Community

The ancient rabbis taught that every Jewish soul—including those of our generation and of future generations—was present at Mount Sinai when the

Torah was given. They also taught that God gave the Torah to the community as a whole and simultaneously to each of us individually, according to our abilities and needs. Therefore, according to Jewish tradition, each of us has received a unique understanding of Torah, one we can share with and teach to others.

Just as God revealed the Torah as we stood together, so are we encouraged to study it together. When we study with our community, we share our special understanding of God's words.

Of course, we can also study by ourselves, and often we do. But when we study in community with others, we can contribute our ideas and learn from others. Together we can struggle with difficult questions, as the ancient sages did, arriving at a new understanding of the sacred texts. The more we learn, the more we have to give, and the stronger we become as individuals and as a community.

Our tradition encourages us to study with people our own age and also with those who are younger and older than we are. What might be one benefit of studying with people of different ages?

IT'S A BALANCING ACT

Many of our blessings and prayers encourage us to remember that we are part of a community. That is why we say, "Blessed are You, *our* God," not "*my* God." That is why we say, "Help *us* lie down in peace," not "Help *me* lie down in peace."

How can attending synagogue services remind you to balance your concern for yourself with your concern for others?

_____

_____

_____

_____

WE PRAY AS A
Community

There are times when we are moved to pray alone. It may happen when we are overcome with feelings of love and gratitude and want to thank God for all the good in our lives or when we feel sad or anxious and want comfort. Those moments of private prayer can hearten and strengthen us.

But when we pray with our community, the doors of opportunity open wider. We are reminded that we are not alone: We are part of a very large family. We are reminded of our responsibility to honor the *Brit*, and we are reminded that we can work together with others to fulfill that responsibility. When we pray as a community, we share the words of our prayer book, words that have been recited for thousands of years by generations of Jews in every part of the world, from Australia to South Africa, from Poland to Israel and the United States. Through the words of the siddur and the rituals of the prayer service, we share the sacred memories and hopes of our people.

Among the skills you can develop in religious school are leading your community in prayer and participating in prayer services.

WE SUPPORT EACH OTHER
as a Community

Jewish tradition is filled with *mitzvot* of celebration—Shabbat, holidays, and joyous events, such as weddings and baby namings. At those times, we come together to share our joy and to give thanks for the goodness in our lives.

Our community also comes together in times of difficulty and sorrow. We reach out to help others—for example, by bringing hot meals to elderly people, visiting the sick, and comforting people whose loved ones have died.

Of course, it's possible to move through the year without celebrating Shabbat in synagogue and to turn thirteen without having led a communal prayer service. And it certainly is possible to do volunteer work alone. But although it is possible, what is lost are valuable opportunities to build a caring community and to take your place in it. What also may be lost are opportunities to accomplish goals that are too great for one person to achieve alone.

You could light a Hanukkah menorah and eat latkes by yourself, but would it be as much fun as celebrating the holiday with others? Why or why not?

Compare the joy of a family and small group of friends attending a life-cycle event with that of an entire community expressing its joy and good wishes for the celebrants. Compare the impact of one person's demanding justice for the poor and oppressed with a community of hundreds—perhaps thousands—of people working together to support the cause. Then you will begin to understand how your participation in a community can make a difference.

CAN YOU BE PART OF THE JEWISH Community yet Different?

"Do not separate yourself from the community" teaches that only by working together can we fulfill the instructions of the Torah. But, you may ask, if we must not separate ourselves from the community, must each of us be the same as everyone else? Must everyone have the same opinions? tastes? personality? Should we not stand up for what we believe if our point of view differs from that of others?

Our sages taught that God makes every person different. Each of us is one of a kind. Not even identical twins or best friends are carbon copies, and certainly the members of a family or community are not exactly the same, no matter how much they have in common. We're all lucky to be different because that's what makes each of us special and able to help and enjoy one another.

A truck, a motorcycle, and a car—even a very unusual looking car—all have something in common: They are forms of transportation. So it is with people. Though we look different, even very different, from one another, we are all made in God's image and can work together to accomplish important goals.

Our differences help make some of us good shortstops, others great infielders, others terrific pitchers, and yet others loyal fans. They enable some of us to use humor to cheer up a friend, others to bring words of comfort, and yet others to offer practical advice. And they motivate some of us to serve on synagogue committees and participate in civil rights rallies, others to visit Israel and teach Hebrew, and yet others to volunteer in animal shelters and contribute tzedakah to the homeless.

Without our differences, life would be dull, perhaps impossible! Too much would be left undone for lack of people with the necessary interests and abilities. If everyone were a professional athlete, who would make movies? build bridges? write software? or plant crops?

But even though we may benefit from our differences, sometimes they can lead to disagreements. You may want to go to the movies when your best friend wants to go swimming. You may crave ice cream when the rest of your family wants cake. Sometimes friends or family members can become impatient or angry when they disagree—for example, about who is responsible for a particular chore or when it should be done.

When that happens, how can remembering the value of our differences help us express our disagreement or feelings in a respectful way? How can it help us listen to others and keep an open mind?

A SPIRIT OF UNITY, KLAL YISRAEL

The spirit of unity in Jewish communities is sometimes called *klal Yisrael*, "the entire Jewish people." *Klal Yisrael* includes every single Jew without exception—every Jew in your family and neighborhood, every Jew in the country and the entire world. Though we may have many different customs, opinions, and experiences, we are one people.

As *klal Yisrael*, we are taught to celebrate our many shared traditions, to be respectful of our differences, and to work together as a holy people, *am kadosh*.

Ancient Stories for Modern Times

THE LIVING LADDER

Once, the Ba'al Shem Tov taught, in a country far, far away, a magnificent bird with a rainbow of feathers nested atop the tallest tree in the land. The king of the country, who was a kind and generous ruler, asked that the bird be brought to him. The people wanted to please the king, so they made a living ladder to reach the bird. Each person stood upon the shoulders of the next until they had almost succeeded.

But it took a long time to build the human, ladder and those who stood nearest the ground lost patience and shook themselves free, and everything collapsed.

If you could have spoken to the people in the story, what might you have said to persuade them to be more patient?

_____

_____

_____

Imagine that the king in the story was God and that the people of the kingdom were the Jewish people. Describe something that God might request that would require us to work patiently together.

_____

_____

MAKE A DIFFERENCE
as a Community

Jewish tradition teaches that the community is greater than any single individual because the community serves everyone. No matter how rich, famous, or intelligent, no one is considered above it. Even Albert Einstein—a genius by any measure—relied on the same farmers for food, construction workers for roads, and firefighters for protection as did other members of his community. In turn, he gave back to the community beyond his professional accomplishments as a physicist. Einstein, a Jewish resident of Princeton, New Jersey, was a human rights activist, a champion of nuclear disarmament, and a fund-raiser for the establishment of the modern State of Israel.

Similarly, Rabbi Abraham Joshua Heschel joined the civil rights movement in the 1960s to fight for justice for African Americans because he believed that "to care for our brother ardently, actively, is a way of worshipping God."

Albert Einstein believed that "the life of the individual has meaning only insofar as it aids in making the life of every living thing nobler and more beautiful."

Increased Responsibility

If a person lives in a town for thirty days, he or she becomes responsible for contributing to the soup kitchen; for three months, to the tzedakah box; for six months, to the clothing fund; for nine months, to the burial fund; and twelve months, to the repair of the town walls. (Talmud, *Bava Batra 8a*)

Why might our tradition teach that the longer you live in a community, the greater your responsibilities to it are?

_____

_____

_____

_____

What do you think Rabbi Heschel meant by that? What does it teach about the Jewish view of our responsibility for the larger, secular community? Rav Yirmiyah taught that a person who works to meet the needs of the community is like one who is occupied with Torah (Jerusalem Talmud, *B'rachot* 5:1, 8d). How might a person's participation in these activities make him or her "like one who is occupied with Torah": volunteering in a shelter for the homeless, visiting residents of a nursing home participating in an interfaith dialogue?

These people are showing their support for Israel by attending an Israel Solidarity Day parade. How is supporting the Jewish homeland like being "occupied with Torah"?

Living in community with others provides us not only with support and friendship but also with the opportunity to make a difference in the lives of others, perhaps even in the lives of future generations. It enables us to help fulfill the *Brit* and make the world a kinder, more just, and more peaceful place.

You have a long and interesting life ahead of you. How many opportunities will you take to join with the community and make a difference?

חָבֵר אָנִי לְכָל־אֲשֶׁר יְרֵאוּךָ

I am the friend of all who revere You.
—Psalm 119:63

LEARN iT & LiVE iT

▶ **1.** Describe one way in which you can support your synagogue community.

_____

_____

_____

_____

▶ **2.** Describe one way in which you can serve your religious school community.

_____

_____

▶ **3.** Describe one way in which you can work with your religious school community to serve others. What mitzvah can you observe with your class or school to help those in need?

_____

_____

▶ **4.** How might serving others be a way of also serving yourself—for example, strengthening yourself?

_____

_____

_____

וְאַל תָּדִין אֶת חֲבֵרְךָ עַד שֶׁתַּגִּיעַ לִמְקוֹמוֹ:

Hillel said, "Judge not your companion until you have been in your companion's place."

—*Pirkei Avot 2:4*

THE VALUE OF
Judging

The witnesses testified, "We saw the accused murderer with a sword in his hand running after the victim. The victim entered a shop and the accused man ran in after him. When we came into the shop, we found the victim lying dead on the floor. In the accused man's hand was the sword, still dripping with blood."

Yet the accused man was acquitted, set free, because the witnesses had not seen the murder take place and so they could not be positive that he had committed the crime.

—Talmud, *Sanhedrin* 37b

When you hear that a friend or classmate has done something wrong—perhaps started a fight or been unkind—what is your reaction? How do you evaluate his or her behavior? Does your decision depend on how well you know or like the person? And how do you know what actually happened—can you assume that what you've heard is true, or do you need to find out the facts for yourself?

WE ARE ALL
Judges

Making judgments is a part of our everyday lives. Think about it. How often do you make judgments about whom to trust, whom to help, whom to befriend, and whom to avoid? How often do you ask yourself, "Is this person a loyal and caring friend? Is she being fair to me? honest? kind?" "Is he reliable? trustworthy? caring?"

Although you don't wear the robes of a courtroom judge, you do serve as a judge when you make such decisions. You have standards for how others should behave—a clown should be funny, a rabbi caring, a teacher knowledgeable, a friend loyal. When people behave as you expect—or when they don't—you often make a judgment: He's not a good clown; she's a great rabbi.

This photograph looks funny because you don't expect a police officer to look like a man-eating fish. What are two qualities you think a good police officer should have?

But how can you learn to judge fairly and honestly without going to law school? How can you be sure that your expectations are fair and reasonable and that your judgments are correct?

If people tried on your shoes—that is, if they put themselves in your place—what would they discover about you? What might they learn about the hard work and effort that go into being you?

TRY ON
Their Shoes

Judaism teaches us to put ourselves in the next person's shoes before passing judgment. In other words, we must try to imagine what we would do were we faced with the same situation and challenges. In that way, we learn to judge

others' behavior as we would want our behavior to be judged.

In the United States, similar thinking requires that in criminal cases people be judged by a jury of their peers (people who come from the same or a similar community and background). For only peers can imagine themselves in the accused person's situation.

When we put ourselves in the next person's place, it is easier to remember that like ourselves, others may make mistakes yet still be good people. That understanding helps us more willingly consider the reasons for a person's behavior: whether there were special circumstances that should be considered and whether the person should be given a second chance. After all, that is what we hope others will do when judging our actions.

SOUND FAMILIAR?

Explain how judging others as you want to be judged is another way of observing the commandment to "love your neighbor as yourself." (Leviticus 19:18)

_____

_____

_____

_____

_____

WHAT'S THE
Proof?

When a teacher or parent reprimands us, most of us want the opportunity to explain our actions, to have that person understand why we did what we did. We want the teacher or parent to consider all the evidence before drawing any conclusions. Therefore, when making judgments ourselves, we, too, must gather and consider all the facts so that we can understand what happened and—equally important—why.

Our tradition requires that judgments be based on reliable evidence. Not gossip, not rumor, and not the appearance of wrongdoing. None of those is reliable evidence. We may think that someone looks or sounds guilty, or we may be influenced by someone's having made similar mistakes in the past. But without proof, we cannot find the person responsible. In fact, according to Jewish law even the slightest doubt, the slightest lack of evidence, should be weighed in favor of a person accused of a wrongdoing.

They say that seeing is believing, but sometimes you need more information than your eyes can deliver. The statue on the right looks like the Statue of Libery, but it's a replica located in Las Vegas, Nevada. So, too, with accusations of wrongdoing. We cannot be satisfied with limited information; we must gather all the relevant facts before deciding whether or not someone is responsible.

Seek and Pursue Justice

The word *tzedek*, "justice," appears twice in Deuteronomy 16:20:

$$\text{צֶדֶק צֶדֶק תִּרְדֹּף}$$

"Justice, justice shall you pursue."

Our sages explained that the first mention of justice is to teach us to seek justice for ourselves; the second is to instruct us to pursue justice for others.

Bible Bio:
The Daughters of Tz'lafeḥad

The Torah teaches that before our ancestors entered the Land of Israel, God instructed Moses to divide the land among the men of the community. But the five daughters of Tz'lafeḥad—Maḥlah, Noah, Ḥoglah, Milkah, and Tirtzah—spoke up, for their father had died, and there was no man in their household. They stood before Moses and the community of elders and pleaded:

תְּנָה־לָּנוּ אֲחֻזָּה בְּתוֹךְ אֲחֵי אָבִינוּ:

"Give us a holding among our father's family.

וַיַּקְרֵב מֹשֶׁה אֶת־מִשְׁפָּטָן לִפְנֵי יהוה: וַיֹּאמֶר יהוה אֶל־מֹשֶׁה לֵּאמֹר: כֵּן בְּנוֹת צְלָפְחָד דֹּבְרֹת נָתֹן תִּתֵּן לָהֶם אֲחֻזַּת נַחֲלָה בְּתוֹךְ אֲחֵי אֲבִיהֶם וְהַעֲבַרְתָּ אֶת־נַחֲלַת אֲבִיהֶן לָהֶן:

"Moses brought their case before Adonai. And Adonai said to Moses, 'The plea of Tz'lafeḥad's daughters is just. You should given them a hereditary holding among their father's family. Transfer their father's share to them.'" (Numbers 27:4–7)

Maḥlah, Noah, Ḥoglah, Milkah, and Tirtzah teach us to speak out when our cause is just.

PURSUE
Justice

The Bible commands every member of the Covenant, every Jew, to pursue justice (Deuteronomy 16:20). Judges are required to decide their cases justly no matter who is involved—Jew or non-Jew, neighbor or stranger, rich or poor (Deuteronomy 1:16–17). And we are all instructed that "to do what is righteous and just is more desired by God than is sacrifice" (Proverbs 21:3).

THE EXTRAORDINARY ACTS OF ORDINARY PEOPLE:
Ruth Bader Ginsburg

Ruth Bader Ginsburg (b. 1933) was sworn in as the 107th justice to the U.S. Supreme Court in 1993. She is the first Jewish woman to serve on the Supreme Court.

Justice Ginsburg grew up in Brooklyn, New York, attended public school, and was confirmed with honors from the East Midwood Jewish Center. On the wall of her court chambers, she has posted the quotation "Justice, justice, shall you pursue" (Deuteronomy 16:20).

In 1996, Justice Ginsburg wrote, "I am a judge born, raised, and proud of being a Jew. The demand for justice runs through the entirety of the Jewish tradition. I hope, in my years on the bench of the Supreme Court of the United States, I will have the strength and courage to remain constant in the service of that demand."

Why does our tradition consider justice so important? One key reason is that the Jewish people have often been oppressed as strangers, as foreigners in other lands. Our people were enslaved in Egypt, imprisoned and slaughtered during the Crusades and the Holocaust, and denied our rights, imprisoned, and murdered in Iran, Argentina, and the former Soviet Union. There was even a time in the United States—not more than seventy years ago—when Jews were frequently denied jobs, housing, and entry into leading universities and social clubs simply because they were Jews.

Because we know what it is like to be outsiders, to suffer because of anti-Semitism, prejudice, and other forms of injustice, our tradition requires that we work hard to add justice, *tzedek*, to the world.

SHOW SOME MERCY, Please

God is both just and merciful. And so as creatures made in God's image, we, too, must balance justice with mercy. That is why our tradition teaches not only that there must be consequences for wrongdoing but also that efforts must be made to soften our judgments.

Imagine that you were taking care of a four-year-old who mistreated the family dog by pulling its tail. What might happen if you did not determine a consequence for the child? What might happen if you determined an extremely harsh consequence—for example, if you refused to feed the child at mealtime? What consequence might balance justice with mercy?

At the Passover seder, we eat special foods, such as bitter herbs and haroset, to remind us of how our ancestors suffered as slaves in ancient Egypt.

This tallit collar, made by Rabbi Vicki Lieberman, includes a quotation from Hosea 2:19. The verse teaches us that God promised to marry the Israelites in righteousness and justice, with goodness, mercy, and faithfulness. What do you think that means?

Ancient Stories for Modern Times

BALANCE JUSTICE WITH MERCY

The story is told of a beggar who borrowed money from a wealthy merchant. It was a large sum of money for the poor man but a small amount for the merchant. Yet when the loan was not repaid, the merchant took the beggar to court.

On the appointed day, the courtroom quickly filled with townspeople, for gossip about the case had spread to one and all. Dressed in a black cap and robe, the judged sat at the front of the room, attentively listening to the proceedings. But the townspeople whispered back and forth to one another: "The merchant doesn't need the debt paid. He has enough money without it." "It's such a trifling amount. Why doesn't he simply forgive the debt as tzedakah?"

"Silence," shouted the judge. "This is my verdict. The beggar must immediately return the money he owes. That is justice, and that is what justice requires."

The townspeople sat in shocked silence. The judge then rose, took off his black judge's cap, and turned it upside down. "Now," he said with a smile, "reach into your pockets and help this poor man pay what he owes our rich neighbor. That is mercy, and that is what mercy requires."

Do you think the judge's verdict was just? Why or why not?

_____

_____

_____

Write an alternative ending to the story, one that shows how you would balance justice with mercy.

_____

_____

_____

_____

_____

What About Me?

Judaism teaches us to judge fairly and balance justice with mercy not only when we judge others but also when we judge ourselves.

List two reasons why you think it is important to treat yourself well in this way.

1. _____

   _____

2. _____

   _____

Sometimes when we feel hurt or lonely, we may judge ourselves or others unfairly. At such times, it can be helpful to find a quiet place to pray for the calm to see our situation more clearly and with more compassion.

Not only does our tradition teach us to balance justice with mercy, but it also teaches us that when we rebuke or reprimand a wrongdoer, we must do so for the sake of the wrongdoer so that he or she will not behave in such a way again. We must not shame the person. Instead, we must speak in a thoughtful and kind way. Going back to the example above, how might you avoid shaming the child who pulled the dog's tail? What might you say, and what tone of voice would you use?

How can remembering the kindness that people have extended to you remind you to treat others with sensitivity and compassion?

WHAT WAS THE KINDEST THING ANYBODY DID FOR YOU TODAY?

THE VALUE OF REBUKE

The Torah instructs us that there are times when it is our responsibility to let others know that they have done something wrong. That includes speaking up when a person is hurtful to others—for example, by gossiping or by playing too aggressively on the sports field. It is also important to speak up when a person is hurtful to himself or herself—for example, by riding a bike without a helmet or not studying for tests.

That teaching is called the value of rebuke, or *tocheiḥah,* meaning "reprimand." The sage Maimonides explained that when we reprimand someone for a wrongdoing, the rebuke should be

- given for the wrongdoer's own good;
- done privately, not in public;
- spoken gently, with concern for the wrongdoer.

Given what you know about the importance that Judaism places on balancing justice with mercy, explain why Maimonides might have insisted that those guidelines be followed when rebuking someone.

_____

_____

_____

_____

_____

_____

Checking Out Our Own Behavior First

Our tradition teaches that before we rebuke someone, we must look at our own behavior. We must ask ourselves whether we are guilty of the same wrongdoing. If we are, first we must correct our own behavior.

Think about the teaching to look at your own behavior and correct it before rebuking someone else. What does it have in common with the teaching to put yourself in someone else's shoes before judging him or her?

_____

_____

_____

_____

How might honoring those two teachings add goodness to the world?

_____

_____

_____

Jewish tradition teaches that when one who judges seeks revenge or personal power, the work of judging becomes destructive. But when a judgment is arrived at fairly, by balancing justice with mercy, the task of judging is constructive and adds goodness to God's world. That is why the sages taught, "For every judge who judges truly, even for an hour, it is counted as if that person had been a partner with God in the work of Creation" (Talmud).

צַדִּיק אַתָּה יהוה

You are just, Adonai.
—Psalm 119:137

LEARN iT & LiVE iT

▶ **1.** List a behavior you dislike in others.

_____

Now think of a time when you were guilty of behaving in that same way. How might remembering that help you be more tolerant and judge others less harshly?

_____

_____

▶ **2.** List a way in which you can pursue justice for yourself—for example, by standing up for yourself when you have been wronged.

_____

List a way in which you can pursue justice for others—for example, by standing up for a classmate who has been wronged.

_____

▶ **3.** Our tradition teaches that just as we balance hot water with cold water to create the temperature that is most pleasing, so must we balance justice with mercy.

If you did not clean up after making a mess in the kitchen, what consequence might your mom or dad devise that would balance justice with mercy?

_____

_____

If a classmate you didn't like acted irresponsibly by breaking your portable CD player, what consequence might you devise to balance justice with mercy?

_____

_____

How would you avoid letting your dislike of the classmate influence you?

_____

_____

תֶּן לוֹ מִשֶּׁלּוֹ שֶׁאַתָּה וְשֶׁלְּךָ שֶׁלּוֹ:

Rabbi Elazar of Bartota says, "Give to God what is God's, because you and all that you have are God's."

—*Pirkei Avot* 3:7

THE VALUE OF
Possessions

Mendel was the richest person in the village of Lem—and the stingiest! On Friday afternoons, when the rabbi came to collect tzedakah for the poor, Mendel gave him but a few copper coins.

One Friday the rabbi asked, "Mendel, what do you see when you look out the window?"

"I see the widow Rifka's house," Mendel answered. "The paint is peeling, most of the windows are broken, and the garden is full of weeds."

The rabbi then pointed to a mirror on the wall and asked, "And what do you see here?"

"Myself," Mendel replied as he looked in the mirror.

"That's interesting," the rabbi said. "Both the window and the mirror are made of glass. The only difference is a thin layer of silver that lines the back of the mirror. But once you add that bit of silver, all you can see is yourself."

—based on *The Dybbuk*, a play by S. Ansky

• •

How much of his or her money do you think a wealthy person should give to tzedakah? Five percent? Ten percent? Twenty percent? Half? Why?

How do you decide how much of your money to save and how much to use for treats, how much to spend on gifts, and how much to give to tzedakah?

Practical

Rabbi Elazar ben Azaryah taught, "If there is no food, there is no Torah; if there is no Torah, there is no food" (*Pirkei Avot* 3:17). Put more plainly, if our bellies are empty, we will be too hungry to concentrate on learning the lessons of Torah, but without the lessons of Torah, our lives will be without meaning.

Are you surprised that the teaching begins with the importance of food rather than with the importance Torah?

Part of what made our ancient sages so wise was that they were realistic—they lived in the real world. They understood that if people do not eat, they will not survive. And if they do not survive, they cannot perform *mitzvot*. The Book of Psalms expresses this in a practical, down-to-earth way: "The dead cannot praise God" (Psalm 115:17).

Our sages understood that the soul needs a different type of nourishment from the body. For example, we nourish our souls when we recite Hamotzi over bread, expressing gratitude to God for the food we are about to eat. Can you read the Hebrew words on the ḥallah board even though they don't have vowels?

FIRST THINGS FIRST

This famous teaching is typical of the practical viewpoint of our sages: "If you are holding a young tree in your hand when you are told that the Messiah has come, first plant the sapling, and then go out to greet the Messiah." (*Avot de Rabbi Natan* 31)

Ancient Stories for Modern Times

A TIME FOR REAPING

For twelve years, Rabbi Shimon bar Yoḥai and his two sons hid from the Romans, who had banned the study of Torah in ancient Israel. Living in a cave, they secretly prayed and studied the Bible. When the Roman emperor died and the decree against the Jews was lifted, the father and his sons left their cave and journeyed to Jerusalem.

As they approached the city, Rabbi Shimon and his sons saw the Jewish farmers tending their fields. Offended that they were farming rather than studying Torah, the father and sons cried, "These people give up eternal life for life here on earth."

The fields were immediately covered in flames, until a voice came forth saying, "Have you left your cave to destroy My world? Is it not more important to live by Torah than to study it? Go back to your cave, and study your ways." (Talmud, *Shabbat* 33b)

Explain the lesson of this story in your own words.

_____

_____

_____

_____

_____

As practical people, the rabbis taught that we should pray only in buildings with windows so that we are reminded of the world beyond the synagogue. That is a world in which work must be done—fields must be plowed, families fed, and the sick and elderly cared for. Once again the sages remind us that if we do not attend to basic human needs, there will be no one to study Torah, no one to pray, no one to celebrate the Jewish holy days.

Similarly, the rabbis understood that part of being human is having a healthy desire to experience pleasure. Our tradition therefore teaches us to enjoy the pleasures of Creation—the perfumed fragrance of a flowering garden, the sweet tang of a sun-ripened peach, the shimmering beauty of a golden sunrise. Those are God's gifts for us to experience and enjoy.

When we go to synagogue on Shabbat, we pray, read from the Torah, and socialize with friends. But when we look out the synagogue windows, we are reminded that after the peace and rest of Shabbat there will be much work to do.

Judaism does not encourage us to deprive ourselves of what we need or what can add to our enjoyment of life. But it does ask us to set limits for ourselves. It requires us to be aware of when our desire for pleasure overruns our willingness to act responsibly,

Did You Know?

Did you know that the Hebrew word *avodah* means both "worship" and "work"?

In the space below, write a poem or draw a picture called "*Avodah*" that expresses the importance of both work and prayer.

IT'S A BLESSING

In the spring, when you stroll through a park or a garden, does your nose tingle with delight as you inhale the fragrance of flowers in bloom? Our ancestors enjoyed those same scents. And through these words, they taught us to transform an everyday pleasure into a sacred act—the mitzvah of expressing gratitude to God by reciting a blessing:

בָּרוּךְ אַתָּה יְיָ אֱלֹהֵינוּ מֶלֶךְ הָעוֹלָם, בּוֹרֵא עִשְׂבֵי בְשָׂמִים.

"Blessed are You Adonai our God, Ruler of the universe, who creates fragrant plants."

and it asks us to honor the needs and rights of others. It asks us to be mindful of when we have enough—enough possessions, enough food, enough money, enough attention—so that we can share the rest with those in need.

HOW MUCH
Is Enough?

How do we know when we have enough? when we have eaten enough food and acquired enough CDs, clothing, jewelry, and computer games? How do we know if we are spending enough time taking care of ourselves or if we have spent too much time and are being selfish? Are we being generous enough or so generous that we put ourselves at risk? For example, if you spent all your time after school working on a tzedakah project and left no time in which to do your homework or get some exercise,

What in nature are you most thankful for? Why? How do you express your appreciation?

would it be appropriate to describe your behavior as generous or as risky?

Which hats in this store window might you want? Why? Which ones do you need? Why?

In fact, it isn't always easy to know when we have enough. Some situations are clear. You need to eat enough food to grow and maintain a healthy body. That could mean a cup of oatmeal with a banana and eight ounces of milk at breakfast. Maybe you could even take an extra helping of fruit or cereal from time to time. But if you often feel stuffed and uncomfortable at the end of a meal, your stomach is telling you that you're eating more than you need.

NEEDS VERSUS WANTS

Sometimes it can be difficult to tell the difference between what we need and what we want. Next to each item below, write either **N** for "need" or **W** for "want." You may label up to eight items a "need." For help deciding, think about how or if you could survive without each item. For example, think about the impact that not having jewelry, CDs, friends, or a place to live would have on your life.

___ Food   ___ Sleep   ___ Love   ___ Family

___ CDs   ___ Friends   ___ Cell phone   ___ Television

___ Computer   ___ Jewelry   ___ Car   ___ Place to live

___ Education   ___ Vacation   ___ Air-conditioning ___ Allowance

Other situations are less clear. You need enough clothing to keep yourself warm and protected, enough so that you don't have to launder everything you own every day and can set some aside for special occasions, such as Passover or a party. Exactly how much is that? It's hard to say. But if you aren't wearing much of what you own, you probably have more than you need.

TO HAVE AND
to Give

When we are young, our parents try to teach us to respect the difference between what is ours and what belongs to others. They also try to teach us to share what we have. The sages described four types of people with different views on possessions:

1. The person who says, "What is mine is mine and what is yours is yours." That is the average person.
2. The person who says, "What is mine is yours and what is yours is mine." That is the uneducated person.
3. The person who says, "What is mine is yours and what is yours is yours." That is the saintly person.
4. The person who says, "What is yours is mine and what is mine is mine." That is the wicked person.

—*Pirkei Avot* 5:10

Discover Your Spending Habits

One way to learn about yourself and what you value is to look at how you spend your money. How much do you spend on entertainment? on tzedakah? on food? on clothing? on gifts? What do your answers tell you about who and what you value? love? honor? respect?

For two weeks, keep a record of how you spend your money, be it an allowance, gift money, or money you earn doing odd jobs.

SAMPLE EXPENSE FORM

ITEM	COST
1 Book	$10.00
Shirt	$24.99
Snacks	$3.49
Total	$38.48

What did you learn about yourself? How might you change your spending habits? Why would you change them?

If you had to pack up your most precious possessions quickly and place them in your backpack, what would you include? Why?

What Do You Think?

The Talmud teaches, "Even a poor person who lives off tzedakah should perform acts of tzedakah."

Why might our tradition require poor people to give tzedakah—to contribute their time and talent, if not their money? Do you think that is just? Why or why not?

_____

_____

_____

_____

_____

_____

The average person respects his or her rights of ownership as well as the rights of others; the uneducated person sees possessions in a topsy-turvy way; the saintly person gives away everything; and the wicked person selfishly grabs everything.

Notice that only people who are described as average balance their needs and rights with those of others. But such people can risk losing their balance by not sharing with others. For our tradition teaches that for the scales of justice to be balanced, it is not enough to refrain from stealing; we must also share what we have with those in need.

CREATE
Balance

The Talmud instructs us to give at least 10 percent of the money we earn each year to tzedakah, but not more than 20 percent, so that we ourselves don't become dependent on the tzedakah of others. That teaching encourages us to create a just balance between caring for ourselves and helping those in need. In fact, the word *tzedakah* comes from the same root as the word *tzedek*, meaning "justice."

Bible Bio: Miriam

Miriam was the sister of Moses and Aaron. When she was young, she helped save Moses' life by watching over him as he lay in a basket on the Nile River until Pharaoh's daughter found him and adopted him as her own son.

The Torah tells us that many years later, after the Israelites crossed the Sea of Reeds:

וַתִּקַּח מִרְיָם הַנְּבִיאָה...אֶת־הַתֹּף בְּיָדָהּ וַתֵּצֶאןָ כָל־הַנָּשִׁים אַחֲרֶיהָ בְּתֻפִּים וּבִמְחֹלֹת:

"Miriam the prophetess . . . took a timbrel in her hand, and all the women went out after her in dance with timbrels." (Exodus 15:20)

At first, it might seem odd that the women had timbrels (hand-held drums or tambourines). After all, the Israelites did not have a lot of time to pack before they fled Egypt, and they must have been able to carry only their most precious possessions on their long journey. But perhaps the women did consider their musical instruments important. Perhaps, as they fled Egypt, they grabbed their instruments, thinking, "We will need to make music to comfort ourselves when we are sad and to help express joy when we are happy."

Do you have a possession that is valuable to you, though it may not be worth a great deal of money? What is it, and why do you value it?

This tapestry by Naomi Hordes shows the prophet Miriam dancing with a timbrel in her hand.

THE EXTRAORDINARY ACTS OF ORDINARY PEOPLE:
Jacob Henry Schiff

Jacob Henry Schiff (1847–1920) was a successful businessman who lived in New York City. He gave tzedakah generously, particularly to help the Jewish community. Among his many charitable acts, Schiff founded Montefiore Hospital in New York and oversaw the creation of the Henry Street Settlement, which to this day offers health care and educational services to those in need.

When Jacob Schiff died, tens of thousands of mourners lined the streets of Manhattan. They came to pay their respects to a man who had shared his wealth with them, given hope to generations of Jewish immigrants, and saved countless lives.

A HOLY PURPOSE IN NOT BELIEVING IN GOD

Rabbi Moshe Leib of Sasov taught, "Everything in Creation has a purpose."

Surprised, one of his students said, "There are those who do not believe in God. Tell me, Rabbi, what purpose can be served by denying that God exists?"

The rabbi smiled and explained, "When you are approached by someone in need, you must imagine that God does not exist. You must act as if you alone can provide for the person's needs." (Martin Buber, *Tales of the Hasidim*)

Why might our tradition teach that it is just—and therefore an obligation—to help those in need rather than that it is simply a nice thing to do? Do you think our sages were right in putting a limit on how much of our money we should give to those in need? Why or why not?

Judaism teaches that we are human beings, not angels. It does not require us to be saints, nor does it want us to become paupers. Judaism simply asks us to enjoy and appreciate what we have and be willing to share a portion of it with those in need. It asks us to be the best human beings we can be by adding justice to the world.

טוֹב־לִי תוֹרַת־פִּיךָ מֵאַלְפֵי זָהָב וָכָסֶף:

Your Torah is more dear to me than thousands of pieces of gold or silver.

—Psalm 119:72

LEARN iT & LiVE iT

 1. Name one of your favorite possessions, and describe why you value it.

_____

Write a blessing expressing your appreciation to God for either the person who gave you that possession or the person who made it. If you made the item yourself, write a blessing expressing gratitude for having the talent and skills to make it.

_____

_____

2. Rabbi Yosei taught, "Let the property of your friend be as dear to you as your own" (*Pirkei Avot* 2:12). Explain that teaching in your own words.

_____

How is this teaching similar to Hillel's "do not do unto others what is hateful to you," and how can it help you be a good friend when you borrow from a friend?

_____

 3. When we collect more stuff than we need, our possessions may start to feel like clutter. Clutter can create an opportunity to give tzedakah. Go through your home or apartment with your family, and gather the items that are clean and in good condition—clothing, toys, furniture, blankets, and appliances—that you no longer use and that you would like to give to people in need.

Contact your local Jewish Federation or another community agency that can distribute the items to families in need, and find out how the items can be picked up or delivered. You and your classmates may even want to organize a Clean Up Your Clutter Week mitzvah project for your grade or your school.

כָּל מַחֲלֹקֶת שֶׁהִיא לְשֵׁם שָׁמַיִם סוֹפָהּ לְהִתְקַיֵּם וְשֶׁאֵינָהּ
לְשֵׁם שָׁמַיִם אֵין סוֹפָהּ לְהִתְקַיֵּם:

Every disagreement that is for the sake of honoring God shall in the end lead to a permanent result, but every disagreement that is not for the sake of honoring God shall not lead to a permanent result.

—*Pirkei Avot* 5:17

THE VALUE OF
Argument

The Talmud tells the story of Rabbi Yoḥanan, whose study partner, Reish Lakish, had died. To comfort Rabbi Yoḥanan, his students found a brilliant new study partner for him.

Several weeks later his students were surprised that their rabbi was more depressed than ever. "Rabbi, why are you so sad?" they asked.

Rabbi Yoḥanan replied, "My new study partner is a great scholar. In fact, he is so brilliant that he can come up with two dozen reasons why my views are correct. But Reish Lakish found two dozen ways to prove that my thinking was wrong. That's what I miss! The goal of studying Torah with others is not to be proved right but rather to learn more."

• •

Have you ever disagreed with someone and convinced him or her that you were right? What did you say to change the person's mind? Has the opposite happened? Has someone ever convinced you that his or her way of thinking was right? Why did you change your mind? Did you benefit from listening to and considering the other person's point of view? Why or why not?

WHY
Disagree?

The Talmud teaches that when people produce coins using a single mold, the coins come out exactly alike. In contrast, although God creates all people from one mold—that of the first human being—each person is different, a unique creation.

Because each of us is unique, our taste in clothes, books, and music will differ from that of our family; the foods, sports, or movies we enjoy may differ from those our classmates enjoy; and some of our beliefs and opinions will differ from those of our closest friends. Yet as we discussed in Chapter 6, "The Value of Community," our differences can be a big plus, for they are not only what make each of us unique, but they are also what enable us to help and enjoy one another.

How can remembering that everyone in your school is one of a kind—that not one of you can be duplicated like a flyer or brochure—help you treat each person with respect?

There are times, however, when our differences may also cause us to feel hurt or upset. For example, sometimes we may feel frustrated if we're the only one in the family who wants pizza rather than Mexican food, or we may feel disappointed when a friend prefers to stay home rather than hang out at the mall, or we may be turned off by a classmate's sense of humor or offended by the actions of a clique at school. What can be done when our differences feel like a pain rather than a plus? when our differences turn into disagreements that can be uncomfortable or upsetting?

ARGUE FOR THE SAKE OF
Honoring God

Our tradition teaches that disagreements can be either *constructive* or *destructive*. A disagreement is constructive when it increases understanding and brings people closer to the truth. A disagreement is destructive when it leads to hurtful words or physical harm, when it fails to increase understanding between people or bring them closer to the truth. Constructive disagreements strengthen relationships and build trust; destructive disagreements damage relationships with others and weaken the bonds of trust.

Any subject—sports, religion, politics, a dress code—can be the source of constructive disagreement. As long as people speak respectfully to one another and are motivated by an interest in sharing their ideas and listening to those of others, there is an opportunity for understanding to be increased and relationships to be strengthened.

Why might someone who is different from you—in age, nationality, education, or religion—be of interest to you?

Similarly, when there is no interest in sharing ideas or speaking respectfully, any subject can become the source of a destructive disagreement.

Sometimes it may seem simpler (and less controversial) never to open your mouths to speak—perhaps just be a mime. But the gift of speech, when used thoughtfully and respectfully, can strengthen relationships and add goodness to the world.

Imagine that you were a member of a computer club. At a weekly meeting, you suggest that your best friend—who has limited experience with computers—be invited to join. One member said, "You've gotta be kidding! Why are we wasting time discussing this when he doesn't know anything?" Another member said, "It would be great to have a new member. Maybe you could help your friend learn more about computers, or he could take an after-school course, and then join our club in the fall."

How might you have responded to the two people? Which of the two was taking a constructive approach? a destructive approach? Why do you think so?

When disagreement can lead to learning, coming closer to the truth, and improving our relationships with others,

Different Jews often observe different customs. For example, at the Passover seder, in some homes the adults hide the afikomen and the children must find it, and in other homes it is the children who hide it and the adults who must find it. But we are one people and therefore share what is most critical: At all seders, we celebrate our people's freedom from slavery in Egypt.

it is not only constructive to disagree, but it is also a mitzvah. We say that such arguments are "for the sake of Heaven," *l'sheim shamayim*, meaning for

THE DESTRUCTION OF THE SECOND TEMPLE

The Talmud teaches that the Second Temple was destroyed because of the causeless hatred that created disharmony in ancient Israel. So unwilling were the Israelites to work together and settle their differences in a constructive way that the Temple, the center of Jewish life, was destroyed.

In every generation, we have the opportunity to explore our differences in a constructive way, a way that can bring us closer together. Rabbi Abraham Isaac Kook, one of the first chief rabbis of modern Israel, taught, "The Second Temple was destroyed because of causeless hatred. Perhaps the Third will be rebuilt because of causeless love."

the sake of honoring God, for they add holiness to our lives by allowing us to treat others with respect and seek greater knowledge of God's world.

Just as there are differences among family members, friends, and classmates, so there are differences among Jews. There are Conservative, Reconstructionist, Reform, Orthodox, cultural, and secular Jews; Jews who believe in God and Jews who do not; those who pray alone, those who pray in a minyan, and those who do not pray at all. Because of our many differences, we may sometimes forget that there is much all Jews share. For example, the Torah belongs to all of us, as does the history of the Jewish people.

How can learning to disagree with other Jews for the sake of honoring God add to the richness of our tradition?

Warning!
DANGEROUS AREA —
KEEP OUT

LEBENSGEFAHR —
BETRETEN VERBOTEN

PELIGRO — NO PASAR

危ない――立入禁止

DO NOT ENTER

If a discussion moves in the direction of a destructive disagreement, imagine a warning sign in your mind, and back away from trouble.

How can it teach us more about Judaism—the many different ways in which we celebrate holidays, conduct prayer services, understand the Torah—and add to our respect for and trust in one another?

USING THE YETZAR HARA
for a Good Cause

Constructive disagreement is a good example of how we can harness the *yetzer hara*, the "evil impulse," for a good cause. Arguments often start due to the influence of the *yetzer hara*, for it is that impulse that tries to separate people from one another. Yet when we turn such arguments to constructive use—for example, by using them to learn something new about another person or to build a more honest friendship—then we are acting for the sake of honoring God.

In such cases, we overcome the influence of the *yetzer hara*, which begins the disagreement, with the *yetzer hatov*, the "good impulse," which helps people draw closer to one another.

Disagreements that both begin and end with the influence of the *yetzer hara* are destructive instead of helpful. They do not lead to growth or to stronger relationships. For example, in a disagreement with your parents that begins and ends with the influence of the *yetzer hara*, you are unlikely to hear anyone's point of view other than your own. Without a good intention to guide the disagreement, it is impossible to reach a good outcome. Without the support of your *yetzer hatov*, you will not be able to disagree honestly and openly, nor will others be able to learn from you.

When we come together with others to discuss Torah, work on a mitzvah project, plan a prayer service or a Purim carnival, hold a political debate, or form a soccer league, what is most important is to create an atmosphere that encourages trust, honesty, and respect. When people sense that there is an openness to new ideas and an acceptance of differences, they are usually more willing to share their opinions and listen to others.

THE **EXTRAORDINARY ACTS OF ORDINARY PEOPLE:**

Bella Abzug

Bella Abzug (1920–1998) was born in the Bronx, in New York City. As a young girl, she played marbles and checkers, traded baseball cards, attended religious school, and joined Hashomer Hatzair, a Zionist youth movement.

Abzug became a lawyer dedicated to defending women's rights and speaking out against racism, prejudice, and the violence of war. In 1970, she became the first Jewish woman to serve in the U.S. Congress.

While in Congress, Abzug introduced bills for comprehensive child care and for measures to expose secret and illegal activities of the CIA and FBI. She lobbied for a nuclear test ban treaty and was a strong supporter of Israel.

In a 1977 Gallup poll, Bella Abzug was named one of the twenty most influential women in the world. Never afraid to speak her mind, she once played off a West African proverb that Theodore Roosevelt liked to quote, "Speak softly but carry a big stick. You will go far." She said, "Woman have been trained to speak softly and carry a lipstick. Those days are over."

Think of a time when you participated in an extended activity with others—a group report, an art project, a team sport. In what ways did you get to know and appreciate one another as time went on? Did you feel comfortable expressing your opinions? Why or why not?

Ancient Stories for Modern Times

WHERE'S THE PROOF?

According to legend, one day when his colleagues would not accept his argument regarding a point of Jewish law, or *halachah*, Rabbi Eliezer cried out, "If *halachah* agrees with me, let this carob tree prove it!" Miraculously, the carob tree was uprooted and replanted a distance away.

But the other rabbis insisted, "No proof can be brought from a carob tree."

Determined, Eliezer countered, "If the *halachah* agrees with me, let the stream of water prove it!" To everyone's amazement, the water began to flow backward.

But the other rabbis stood firm: "No proof can be brought from a stream of water."

Eliezer and the others went back and forth until finally Eliezer shouted, "If the *halachah* agrees with me, let it be proved from heaven!"

No sooner had he said this than a divine voice cried out, "Why do you argue with Rabbi Eliezer, with whom the *halachah* always agrees?"

But Rabbi Joshua stood up and protested, "*Lo vashamayim hi!* 'The Torah is not in heaven!' [Deuteronomy 30:12]. God gave it to us at Mount Sinai."

Some time later Rabbi Natan met the prophet Elijah and asked him, "What did the Holy One do in that moment when Rabbi Joshua spoke up?" Elijah answered, "God laughed with joy, saying, 'My children have bested Me, My children have bested Me.'"

What lesson might our tradition want to teach when it tells us that God took pleasure in Rabbi Joshua's response?

_____

_____

_____

_____

מָה־אָהַבְתִּי תוֹרָתֶךָ כָּל־הַיּוֹם הִיא שִׂיחָתִי׃

How I love Your Torah; I debate it all day long.
—Psalm 119:97

LEARN iT & LiVE iT

▶ **1.** Create a list of three important rules for arguing constructively.

A. _____

B. _____

C. _____

▶ **2.** List two things you might say or do to help turn a destructive disagreement into a constructive disagreement.

A. _____

B. _____

▶ **3.** Write a motto or saying that can serve as a reminder to argue constructively rather than destructively. For example, "Use words to build relationships, not to tear them down."

_____

_____

Illustrate your motto or saying.

הֱוֵי מִתַּלְמִידָיו שֶׁל אַהֲרֹן אוֹהֵב שָׁלוֹם וְרוֹדֵף שָׁלוֹם אוֹהֵב אֶת הַבְּרִיּוֹת וּמְקָרְבָן לַתּוֹרָה:

Hillel said, "Be one of the students of Aaron, loving peace and pursuing peace, loving people and drawing them near to Torah."

—Pirkei Avot 1:12

THE VALUE OF
Peace

One day a rabbi walked through the market- place and spied the prophet Elijah, who, tradition teaches, will announce the coming of the Messiah. The rabbi asked Elijah, "Who among these people is worthy of a special place in the world to come?"

"None," responded Elijah.

A moment later two men walked past them. They smiled and greeted everyone they passed. "These men will have a share in the world to come," said Elijah to the rabbi.

Wondering what was so special about them, the rabbi approached the two men, saying, "I have heard that you are exceptionally worthy. Why is that said of you?"

They modestly responded, "Surely we are not unusually worthy. We simply try to cheer those who are sad and help make peace between those who quarrel."

—Talmud, *Ta'anit* 22a

Think of a time when you felt peaceful. Were you alone or with family; were you at home, in synagogue, or outdoors? What made you feel peaceful? What can you do to feel that way again?

A TRADITION
of Peace

Symbols of peace, *shalom*, are found throughout Jewish tradition. Shabbat is known as a day of peace that celebrates harmony among people, God, and nature. One of God's names is *Oseh Shalom*, "Peacemaker." And the Temple in Jerusalem was a monument to peace where Jews prayed for their own well-being and for the well-being of other nations.

In Hebrew, we wish each other peace each time we say hello and good-bye.

In fact, from the time of the Bible, *shalom* has been an important value, one that is rich with meaning. Not only does *shalom* mean "the absence of war," but it also means "safety," "wholeness," "completion," "fulfillment," "prosperity," "health," and "peace of mind and heart."

That is why our tradition teaches us not only to speak words of peace to those who quarrel but also to provide food, shelter, and medicine to those who suffer from war's violence and destruction. And that is why our tradition teaches that until all God's creatures live in peace and safety, the world cannot be whole, and none of us can enjoy complete peace of mind and heart.

PEACE IS ALWAYS IN OUR PRAYERS

As Jews, we pray for peace throughout our day and week. When we recite the Amidah, we pray that God will "grant peace to the world, with goodness and blessing, grace, love, and mercy." When we sing Birkat Hamazon, "Grace After Meals," we ask that God "cause peace to dwell among us." And when we say the Hashkiveinu prayer, we ask God to "spread over us the shelter of Your peace."

וּבַמָּקוֹם הַזֶּה אֶתֵּן שָׁלוֹם

חגי ב:ט

في هذا المكان أُعطي السلام

حجي اصحاح ٩:٢

And in this place I will give Peace

Haggai 2:9

This quotation from the prophet Haggai hangs in the Tower of David in Jerusalem. Jerusalem is sometimes called the City of Peace.

Just as we are taught not to wait until we have leisure time to study Torah, for we may never have leisure time, so are we taught not to wait for special occasions to seek peace. Instead, we must pursue peace as a regular part of our daily lives. In fact, as Jews one of our main responsibilities is to pursue peace—to sow seeds of peace within ourselves, our families, and the Jewish people, as well as in the larger world.

The following tips can help you pursue peace for yourself:

- **Find a quiet corner, and recite a prayer.** When you are upset, compose your own request for peace and calm or recite a prayer from the prayer book. For example, you might say, "Dear God, please comfort and protect me so that I may find peace."

- **Find a trustworthy "sounding board."** Speak to an adult or a peer who will listen respectfully to your concerns and perhaps make helpful suggestions.

- **Keep a diary or journal.** Recording you thoughts and actions, even your dreams, can help you think about the people and activities that help you feel at peace.

THERE'S NO PLACE
Like Home

Rabbi Shimon ben Gamliel taught, "Those who make peace in their homes are as if they made peace in all Israel" (*Avot de Rabbi Natan* 28:3).

Why might peace in the home, *sh'lom bayit*, be considered so important? How might adding peace in your home have an impact on peace *outside* your home?

Sometimes we can enjoy the company of family members even when we're just quietly doing our own thing—reading or playing video games—in the same room. Although we may speak only occasionally at such times, there is a special sense of shalom and pleasure in being in one another's company.

Think about it. How do your family relationships affect your relationships outside your home? On days when you leave your house with a hug or a smile, is your behavior different from what it is on days when you've had a quarrel with your mom or dad? Why? And does the quality of your day at school affect your behavior at home? If you strike out three times in baseball, or play a sour note in orchestra, or lose your favorite pen, how do you react when you get home?

By first learning to live peaceably with those we love (which can be more difficult than you might think!), we can establish an island of *shalom* that slowly extends beyond our home. We develop confidence in ourselves, trust in others, and the willingness to talk through our differences.

SHABBAT SHALOM

On Shabbat, we try to let go of the tensions of the week so that *shalom* can fill the day. What can you do on Shabbat to help make your home a more peaceful and loving place?

One way to remind yourself and others of the importance of *sh'lom bayit* is to greet the members of your family with the traditional words for saying hello and good-bye on the holiest day of the week: "*Shabbat shalom.*"

Here are a few tips that can help you pursue peace at home (and outside your home!) when things get a bit stressful:

- **Speak respectfully.** Being rude won't get you what you want. It will just make others feel mistrustful and defensive.

- **Listen to what others have to say.** Don't get so caught up in proving you are right that you don't hear what's bothering the other person.

- **Be patient.** If you cannot resolve a conflict with someone, suggest that you each give things a rest and return to the issue at a later time.

Sometimes family members may disappoint one another (as we all disappoint ourselves at times). But as long as we make a sincere effort to listen to others' points of view and needs, and as long as we work hard to improve our own attitudes and behavior, then *sh'lom bayit* will be a realistic goal.

The beauty and warmth of the Shabbat table remind us that the seventh day of the week is special. We may not succeed in living peacefully 24/7, but we can do our best to make our homes islands of peace on Shabbat.

It Happens in Every Family

Let's be honest: *Every* family has its problems and conflicts. Our patriarch Jacob tricked his brother, Esau, *and* his father, Isaac; our matriarch Leah was jealous of her younger sister, Rachel; and King David and his children had many problems getting along. Fortunately, the Torah doesn't require families to be perfect; it requires only that all members of the family do their best to pursue peace.

Kids sometimes complain that their parents make demands on them—to do a chore, home-work, or an errand—just when they are ready to relax. Does that ever happen to you? Think about what you can do to avoid turning a parent's request into a family conflict.

What I can do to avoid family conflicts:

_____
_____

_____

What I'd like my parents to do to avoid such conflicts:

_____

_____

_____

How I'll let my parents know what I'm thinking:

_____

_____

_____

The Entire Jewish People—Klal Yisra'el

Klal Yisra'el **includes every single Jew in the world without exception—every Jew in your family, synagogue, and neighborhood; every Jew in North America, South America, Europe, and the Middle East. We are one people no matter where we live.**

As *klal Yisra'el,* **we are taught to celebrate our many shared traditions, to be respectful of our differences, and to work together as members of the Covenant.**

PURSUE PEACE IN THE
Jewish Community

At every prayer service, we recite the Kaddish prayer. Its final words ask for God's help in making peace in our homes and in the Jewish community: "May the Maker of Peace, who makes peace over the universe, make peace among us and all of Israel."

The Talmud's teaching that the Second Temple was destroyed as a result of the causeless hatred that created disharmony in ancient Israel (see page 112) is a reminder of the importance of peace within the Jewish community.

But it is not always easy to get along with others. Though we may all be Jews, we are still different, and therefore we often have different points of view, different habits, and even different beliefs and customs. That is why the Bible teaches, "Seek peace and pursue it" (Psalm 34:15). For not only must we look for peace, but we also must run after it with all our might, because it can easily slip away.

Attending Shabbat services, going to religious school, and participating in a synagogue food drive for the needy are just a few ways in which you can help pursue peace in the Jewish community. For when Jews come together to pray, study Torah, and perform acts of tzedakah and lovingkindness, we are reminded of the purpose of our community: to help make the world a more just and more peaceful place.

Volunteering to take pictures at special synagogue events—such as Purim carnivals, model seders, and musical performances—is not only fun but also a good way to be of service and to strengthen your ties to the Jewish community.

Sometimes our words and actions send mixed messages—for example, we might welcome new students with friendly words but then ignore them in the playground. What actions can you take to send a clear, welcoming message to a new classmate?

Here are a few tips to help you add peace to the Jewish community:

- **Be welcoming.** When someone new joins your class or synagogue, say hi and introduce yourself. (Remember what it felt like to be the new kid in your neighborhood, class, or bunk at camp? At such times, how does it feel to have a friendly person reach out to you?)

- **Don't gossip or spread rumors.** Gossiping is a hurtful practice that undermines trust and harmony. Strong as the impulse to gossip may sometimes be, the good impulse, *yetzer hatov*, can help you overcome the temptation.

- **Find constructive ways to interact with the Jewish community.** By participating in mitzvah projects, junior congregation, and special holiday events, such as Purim carnivals, you will come to know more people and develop common goals and interests. The more you participate, the stronger the relationships within your community will become.

ADD PEACE
to the World

The world is a very good, though imperfect, place. At any moment, thousands of kind and generous acts—both small and great—are performed by people of different ages, religions, races, and ethnicities. Even as you read this sentence, somewhere in the world a Hindu doctor is performing surgery on a Christian patient; a teenager is teaching an elderly woman to read; a soldier has laid down his gun to help a frightened child.

Bible Bio: The Prophet Isaiah

The prophet Isaiah (Isaiah ben Amoz) was born in Jerusalem about two hundred years before the destruction of the First Temple. Though the Israelites often fought among themselves and strayed from God's path of righteousness, Isaiah persisted in his efforts to guide them toward peace and justice. His inspiring words describe a time when all the nations of the world will live together in peace:

וְכִתְּתוּ חַרְבוֹתָם לְאִתִּים וַחֲנִיתוֹתֵיהֶם לְמַזְמֵרוֹת לֹא־יִשָּׂא גוֹי אֶל־גּוֹי חֶרֶב וְלֹא־יִלְמְדוּ עוֹד מִלְחָמָה:

"And they shall beat their swords into plowshares and their spears into pruning hooks; nation shall not lift up sword against nation, neither shall they learn war anymore." (Isaiah 2:4)

THE EXTRAORDINARY ACTS OF ORDINARY PEOPLE:
Yitzḥak Rabin

Yitzḥak Rabin (1922–1995) was a military commander who served in the defense of Israel for twenty-seven years and then became prime minister. In 1993, Rabin signed a peace treaty with Yasir Arafat, chairman of the Palestine Liberation Organization. Rabin heeded the words of the prophet Isaiah when he signed the treaty and said, "Let us pray that a day will come when we will say: 'Farewell to arms.'"

On November 4, 1995, a rally was held in Tel Aviv in support of the peace process. As it came to an end, from a high platform, Yitzḥak Rabin joined the crowd in singing "The Song of Peace":

So sing only a song for peace
Do not whisper a prayer
Better sing a song for peace
With a great shout.

When the song ended, Rabin left the platform. As he walked toward his car, he was shot and killed by Yigal Amir, a Jew who opposed the peace process.

At the same time, there also is much work to be done to repair and improve the world. Wars scar the lives and land of innocent people; diseases and famines bring pain and suffering to those already oppressed by poverty's harshness; and children who are too hungry and cold to have pleasant dreams lie awake at night.

Each time you work to bring peace between people who quarrel, comfort someone who is ill, make a friend of a former enemy, or donate tzedakah to people who need food or shelter, you help improve the world and make it a bit more peaceful and whole.

Ancient Stories for Modern Times

TURN AN ENEMY INTO A FRIEND

A story is told about Samuel Ibn Nagrela, an eleventh-century Jewish poet who was a close friend of the king of Spain, a Muslim. Jealous of the friendship between the two, a Muslim poet came before the king and falsely accused Ibn Nagrela of stealing one of his poems.

When told of the charges, Ibn Nagrela showed the two men the many drafts of the poem that he had written. "All of my work is here for you to see how, step-by-step, I wrote and revised the poem."

"And can you show me your drafts?" asked the king of the other poet.

"There are none," he sheepishly admitted.

"Then your punishment will be delivered by the hands of Ibn Nagrela," declared the king. And turning to his friend, he continued, "Cut out this man's evil tongue, as he surely would have cut out yours."

Later that day the king passed the room of Ibn Nagrela and heard the sounds of merriment. He opened the door and was surprised to find the two poets laughing and chatting.

"Ibn Nagrela, this man is your enemy. Why have you not removed his evil tongue?" said the bewildered king.

"But I have, Your Majesty," Ibn Nagrela replied. "I have removed his evil tongue and replaced it with a kind one."

How did Ibn Nagrela remove the other poet's evil tongue and replace it with a kind one?

_____

_____

_____

_____

_____

Here are a few tips to help you add peace to the world:

- **Broaden your circle of friends.** The best way to develop an appreciation of the differences between people and to learn to get along with others is to get to know a diverse group of people. You may even want to correspond with a pen pal from another country.

- **Avoid media that present violence as entertainment.** Boycott movies, television programs, and computer games that portray violence as glamorous and exciting.

- **Follow the news.** Get in the habit of following the news in newspapers and magazines or on television, radio, or the Internet. When you understand the issues that affect the world around you, you can make better decisions about what you can do to help make the world a more peaceful place.

The Hebrew words in this photo mean "we are all as one." Not only must Israel and the United States work together for peace, but all people across the globe must do so as well, for we are all part of Creation; we are all as one.

- **Contact your government representatives.** If there is an issue about which you deeply care, e-mail or snail mail your local or national representatives, expressing your concerns.

The Book of Proverbs teaches that the ways of Torah "are pleasant and all her paths are peaceful" (3:17). As a partner in the *Brit*, you have been given the Torah as your sacred path leading to peace. Each act commanded by Torah—such as being honest, respectful, kind, just, and generous—can help you add peace and fulfillment to the world and, most especially, to your own life and the lives of those you love.

How might teaching people of other religions about Judaism help add shalom to the world? What two things about Judaism would you most want to teach? Why?

שָׁלוֹם רָב לְאֹהֲבֵי תוֹרָתֶךָ

There is great peace to those who love your Torah.
—Psalm 119:165

LEARN iT & LiVE iT

▶ **1.** Imagine that you are making a patchwork quilt to cover your family in a shelter of peace. List four values you need to develop within yourself in order to contribute to peace in your home.

_____

_____

Now write the name
of one value in each
of the quilt's squares,
and decorate the squares
so that they can become
part of a beautiful shelter
for peace.

▶ **2.** After negotiating the peace agreement with Yasir Arafat, Israeli prime minister Yitzḥak Rabin commented, "I would have liked to sign a peace agreement with Holland, or Luxembourg, or New Zealand. But there was no need to . . . . One does not make peace with one's friends. One makes peace with one's enemy." What do you think Rabin meant?

_____

How might it apply to your life?

_____

אִם אֵין אֲנִי לִי מִי לִי? וּכְשֶׁאֲנִי לְעַצְמִי מָה אֲנִי? וְאִם לֹא עַכְשָׁיו אֵימָתַי?

If I am not for myself, who will be for me? But if I am only for myself, what am I? And if not now, when?

—*Pirkei Avot* 1:14

THE MATTER OF Balance

There once was a king who granted his people land but taxed them without mercy. One day a wise woman went to the king to ask him to lighten the tax burden on his people. The king refused. The woman said, "If you will not help your people, at least grant me the favor of going boating with me. I have a very comfortable boat."

The king agreed to go with her, and the two set out on the lake. When they arrived at the deepest part, the woman took out a drill and began to bore a hole in the boat. Stunned, the king cried out, "What are you doing? We shall drown."

"Do not be alarmed," said the woman. "I'm drilling only on my side."

After a moment, the king smiled and said, "I understand. As we are in this boat together, so are we in the world together. I must fix the hole I've made with my selfishness before my entire kingdom is lost."

—based on the lesson of Rabbi Shimon bar Yoḥai, *Leviticus Rabbah* 4:6

Each of us changes our point of view throughout the day, focusing at times on our own concerns and at times on those of others. When the rhythm of change feels natural and steady, we may feel pretty good. But sometimes we may feel as if we're walking a tightrope. Shifting from side to side, we may feel ourselves pulled toward an extreme and find it difficult to regain our balance.

At such times, how can we remember to be for ourselves but not only for ourselves, to care for others but not at the expense of our own well-being?

OUR TRADITION
Guides Us

Among Judaism's greatest heroes are those who were able to care for themselves *and* for others. For example, the Torah teaches that when Moses' life was in danger in Egypt, he took care of himself by escaping to Midian. The Torah then tells how Moses left the comfort of his new home to lead the Israelites out of slavery in Egypt. Similarly, the Scroll of Esther teaches how Queen Esther not only took care of herself in King Ahashverosh's court by hiding her Jewish identity but also saved the Jews of ancient Persia by eventually revealing her true identity.

Queen Esther accuses Haman of masterminding the plot to destroy her people, the Jews.

This woman is enjoying a conversation with her friend, but because she is holding her cell phone, she is endangering the lives of others. What would you suggest she do to balance her desire to chat with her friend with her obligation to drive safely?

Ancient Stories for Modern Times

GOOD INTENTIONS

Sometimes even though our intentions are good—for example, we study and seek to do the right thing—we still make mistakes. Our sages understood that, so they shared this story about Rabbi Akiva:

Once Rabbi Akiva found a corpse lying on the roadside far from town. He dragged the corpse to the nearest cemetery and buried it there. When he explained to the other rabbis what he had done, they told him that he had not acted according to the law. The law states that when a corpse is found with no explanation in a strange place, it should be buried there.

"I acted with the best of intentions," lamented Akiva, "and yet I have sinned."

Jewish tradition includes the stories of our heroes' mistakes as well as their achievements. Why are both valuable parts of our tradition?

_____

_____

_____

_____

_____

As you have learned, Jewish heroes are not perfect. They are human and flawed yet worthy models of goodness whom we can strive to be like. That is why Jewish tradition teaches that everyone, not only heroes, must balance their needs and interests with those of others. And that is why the Torah teaches, "Love your neighbor as yourself." For that simple rule is a reminder that not only must we be loving to ourselves, but we must also treat others with respect and extend a helping hand when one is needed.

It is also why many of the Talmud's lessons include detailed instructions on how to live a balanced life—to pursue peace and justice for ourselves

Bible Bio: The Prophet Elijah

We learn about the prophet Elijah in the books of 1 and 2 Kings, as well as from the stories of the ancient rabbis and Jewish folklore. Elijah is often described not only as a man of faith but also as a man of action—a peacemaker and a protector of children, the poor, and the righteous. Tradition teaches that he is present at every Passover seder and *brit milah* (circumcision) and that he will announce the coming of the Messiah, the coming of the age of peace and plenty for the whole world.

We recite Elijah's declaration of faith at the end of the Yom Kippur prayer service:

יהוה הוּא הָאֱלֹהִים:

"Adonai alone is God." (1 Kings 18:39)

and for strangers, to rest on Shabbat *and* to permit other creatures to rest, to enjoy the riches in our lives *and* to share them with those in need.

Happily, many of our actions have a built-in balance. When we take responsibility for eating healthful foods, dressing warmly in cold weather, and getting enough sleep, we not only care for ourselves, but we also relieve our parents of some of the responsibility of caring for us. When we study and participate in class discussions, we not only help ourselves do well in school, but we also enrich the classroom discussion. And when we develop our skills in music or sports, we not only strengthen

When we or others make mistakes, we may sometimes think, "That was a monstrous thing to do." But the Torah teaches us that our mistakes are usually human, not monstrous, and that by taking responsibility for them, we can almost always correct them.

ourselves, but we also add to the enjoyment and success of others—for example, the members of our band or soccer team.

When we feel pulled to an extreme—to disregard either our own needs and interests or those of others—it is time to take a fresh look at ourselves and the world around us. Just as the windows in a synagogue remind us that there is a world beyond the house of prayer—a world where work must be done and justice pursued—so can our eyes be windows that help our souls notice when someone else is hurting or tired or hungry. They can help our souls see opportunities to regain balance, take better care of ourselves, and respond to the needs of others.

TRANSFORM WISDOM
into Action

Judaism encourages us to study the wisdom of our ancestors throughout our lives, to continually make new meaning from it based on our times and on our growing understanding, and then to turn our understanding into action. When we are young, we learn the word *tzedakah* and the importance of sharing what we have, and we turn our

THE EXTRAORDINARY ACTS OF ORDINARY PEOPLE:

Tovah Lieberman

Tovah Lieberman loves the comfort of snuggling under one of the fun quilts her mom has made. Thinking that other kids might also take pleasure in colorful, fun quilts, she chose to mark her becoming a bat mitzvah by making quilts for young children with life-threatening illnesses.

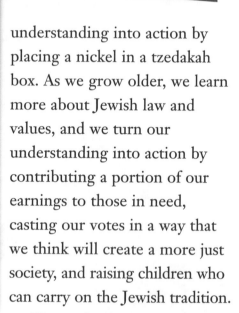

Tovah worked on her project for a year, learning to use a sewing machine, to buy, prepare, and cut quilting fabric, and to follow a pattern. By year's end, she had completed four quilts.

The day of her bat mitzvah ceremony, Tovah displayed the quilts in her synagogue, Bnai Amoona in St. Louis, Missouri. A guest asked Tovah if she would be willing to give one of the quilts to a seventeen-year-old boy with leukemia, whom the guest knew personally. Tovah said yes, though she worried that a teenage boy might find it small and childish.

We often don't know what impact our acts of kindness have on others. But Tovah didn't have to wonder for long. Soon after she sent the quilt, Tovah received a thank-you note from the young man, expressing his gratitude. He was deeply touched by her gift and was saving it for his upcoming hospitalization.

"It felt so good to know that something I did was important to someone else, someone who doesn't even know me!" Tovah said with pride.

understanding into action by placing a nickel in a tzedakah box. As we grow older, we learn more about Jewish law and values, and we turn our understanding into action by contributing a portion of our earnings to those in need, casting our votes in a way that we think will create a more just society, and raising children who can carry on the Jewish tradition.

You and your generation are the inheritors of this tradition. Now it is your turn to study, make meaning, and take action. As you go on your journey, may you find many companions, may you be blessed, and may you be a blessing.

עֵת לַעֲשׂוֹת לַיהוה

It is a time to take action for Adonai.
—Psalm 119:126

LEARN iT & LiVE iT

▶ **1.** Describe something new you learned about one Jewish value as a result of studying *Count Me In*.

_____

_____

_____

How can you use this new understanding to take an action that shows concern for yourself?

_____

_____

How can you use this new understanding to take an action that shows concern for others?

_____

_____

▶ **2.** Describe a situation in which your eyes were your soul's windows. What did your eyes help your soul see? What action did you take?

_____

_____

_____

▶ **3.** Draw a picture or write a poem that describes how you feel when you balance concern for yourself with concern for others.

THE MESSIAH IS READY
When We Are

A legend teaches that long ago in ancient Rome, Rabbi Joshua ben Levi once met the prophet Elijah and asked him, "When will the Messiah come?"

Elijah answered, "Go and ask the Messiah himself."

Startled, Rabbi Joshua asked, "But where will I find the Messiah?"

"At the gates of the town," responded Elijah.

"How will I recognize him?" the rabbi asked.

"He is sitting among the poor lepers," answered Elijah.

So the rabbi went to the gates of the town, and there he found the Messiah. Respectfully, he asked, "When will you come, master and teacher?"

"Today," the Messiah answered.

Rabbi Joshua returned to Elijah, who asked, "What did the Messiah tell you?"

"He spoke falsely, for he said that he would come today, but he has not come," complained the rabbi.

Elijah answered, "This is what he told you: 'Today—if you will but hear My voice'" [Psalm 95:7].

—Talmud, *Sanhedrin* 98a

Each time we hear God's voice and through our actions respond, "*Hineni*. Count me in," the Messiah draws one step closer.

Index